Italia

Jo Seagar

Italia

Jo Seagar

Simple recipes from the Italian Cook School

Photography by Jae Frew

RANDOM HOUSE
NEW ZEALAND

A RANDOM HOUSE BOOK published by
Random House New Zealand
18 Poland Road, Glenfield, Auckland, New Zealand

For more information about our titles go to www.randomhouse.co.nz

www.joseagar.com, www.jaefrew.com

A catalogue record for this book is available from the
National Library of New Zealand

Random House New Zealand is part of the Random House Group
New York   London   Sydney   Auckland   Delhi   Johannesburg

First published 2011

© 2011 recipes Jo Seagar, photographs Jae Frew

The moral rights of the author have been asserted

ISBN 978 1 86979 592 4

Design and photography: Jae Frew
Printed in China by Everbest Printing Co Ltd

This book is dedicated to two special people.

Firstly to Fenisia Vittori. Heartfelt thanks, Mamma, for all your wise words
and advice both culinary and other.

Secondly, to my extraordinary best friend and bridesmaid, Trish Craig.
You are always encouraging, always there for me, so funny, so sensible and
such an inspiration.

Contents

Introduction

I'm quite sure I must have been Italian.

The first fledgling meal I ever prepared solo was Spaghetti Bolognaise — and I adore red handbags and shoes! What more proof do you need?

I know I was made in New Zealand. My family have lived here for generations. I grew up in Hawke's Bay and Auckland. Had formal cooking training in London and Paris. Honed my skills and cleaned lots of ovens in restaurants and cafés. Now I wave my wire whisk and hold a conversation at the same time in Oxford, North Canterbury, but . . . I think I actually came of culinary age in the beautiful little Umbrian village of Eggi under the watchful eye and tutelage of Mamma Fenisia Vittori.

I am about to make my annual visit to Villa Campo Verde for another little fix of Mamma's expertise. There is a tingling of excitement and anticipation deep in my bones. I've searched the wispy thread lines of my own family tree and see absolutely no connection to Italy at all, but I know it's more than wishful thinking. The feeling I get when I return to Mamma — we are connected. We're of the same recipe, Mamma and I. We're family.

Italians are crazily obsessed with food. They talk endlessly about it. At one meal they are planning the next. They discuss where to source food, where to buy it, who is best at preparing this thing or that, what's in season and who makes the best version of traditional dishes.

Continued

Italians regard quality and freshness as paramount — far more important than diversity and innovation.

La Cucina Italia remains distinctly regional and the essence of the cooking is simplicity. Food knowledge is passed down from generation to generation. They seek out the very best that the region and season has to offer. They treat the food with respect and care. And then cook it with Italian passion and heart.

This, for a country girl from New Zealand who loves to drink and eat and cook and laugh and make merry, was music to my ears.

Meeting Mamma and being welcomed by her into the kitchen at Villa Campo Verde was a linking of two like-minded souls. It is such a pleasure spending time with her. She generously shares her knowledge, her methods, her secret recipes, tips and folklore.

This book is my own interpretation of her family recipes and ideas. Italian food is too diverse a subject for any book to be a complete authority but this is my take on the subject. I've written for people who have come home from a trip to Italy or even home from a great meal at an Italian restaurant, wishing they knew how to recreate that deliciousness in their own kitchen.

I know from my previous books and teaching at our cooking school that there is a hunger for culinary knowledge and most importantly, inspiration.

In this book I am sharing not only the recipes Mamma has taught me and things I have learnt on my Italian travels, but also the little hints and handy tips Mamma has passed on. The fine details and wisdom and wit. I hope I do her justice.

At the heart of all cooking, but especially Italian cooking, no matter how rich or poor you are, is the spirit of conviviality. The pleasure that comes from breaking bread together and sharing a meal with those you love.

Buon Gusto

Jo Seagar

Umbria

Italian cooking reflects that the country was only unified in 1861. Until then each region was like a separate little country producing its own characteristic cuisine and relying on what it could gather, cultivate or rear locally.

Umbria is the landlocked heart or centre of Italy and has, for centuries, been the cross-roads for many peoples and cultures. Umbria's oak woods, clear streams and rich volcanic soils yield many delicacies. Chief among these are truffle, trout, olive oils, prized lentils from Castelluccio, cured meats from Norcia, tangy mountain cheeses and beautiful wines.

The cook school is based in a little village called Eggi near Spoleto, a leisurely two-hour drive north of Rome.

GAUL

Pedusa R.

Classes

Forum Cornelii

Srailus R. (Vatrenus R.)

Faventia

Forum Livii

Forum Popilii

Solona

Rubicon R.

Mutilum

Caesena

Ariminus R.

Ariminum

In Castello

Mevaniola

Crustumium R.

M Utis

Bedesis R.

Sarsina

Pisaurum

Signus R.

Faesulae

Arnus R.

Pitinum Pisaurense

Faum Fortunae (Iulia Fanestris)

Ager Senonus

Ad Aquilam

Sestinum

Urbinum

Forum Sempronii (furlo P.)

Sena R.

Sena Gallica

Finesa

Metaurus R.

Aesis R.

Ancona

Bituriia

Pitinum Mergens

Visor R.

Aesis

Camerum Pr.

Cales

Arretium

Tifernum Tiberinum

Sentinum

Ausimum

Numana

Miscus R.

Sena Iulia

Iguvium

Cingulum

Trea

Picina

Flusor R.

Potentia

Cortona

Helvillum

Attidium

Septem

Mosilica

Veda

Camerinum

Urbs Salvia

Cluentus R.

Pausulae

Tinna R.

Castellum

Ad Novas

L. Trasimenus

Perusia

Nuceria

Firmum

Asisium

Falerio

Clusium

Vettona

L. Umber

L. Plestinus

Cupra

Hispellum

Fulginium

Ascuum

Mevania

Trebia

Nar R.

Nursia

Mt. Terrica

Tuder

Spoletium

Volsinii vet. novi

Carsulae

Interamna

L. Velinus

Interamnia

L. Volsiniensis

Ameria

Gurgures Mts.

Pinna

Materum

Visentium

Ferentinum

Narnia (Nequinum)

Reate

Interocrium

Mt. Fiscellus

Vola

L. Vadimonis

Horta

Ocriculum

Foruli

Amiternum

Tuscana

Forum Cassii

Mt. Ciminius

Junonia Falisca

Aquae Cutiliae

Ceraunii Mts.

Aveia

Peltuinum

Aufinum

Blera

L. Ciminius

Valerii

Mt. Soracte

Suana

Volci

Nepete

Feronia

Trebula Mutuesca

Alba Fucens

Ferentum

Sabate

Cures

Eretum

Paeligni

Centumcellae

Castrum novum

Caere

Veii

Nomentum

Crustumerium

Varia

Carsioli

Marruvium

Aequi

ADRIATIC

UMBRIA

PICENUM

ETRURIA

This is a book for anyone who's returned from travels in Italy and wished they could recreate that special feeling back at home.

POST OFFICE
MAURITIUS
ONE PENNY
Villa Campo Verde
Italiano

Italian Pantry

Olive Oil

Italians usually buy their olive oil from someone they know — a local producer or a shop that deals directly with local producers.

When you are buying olive oil, how can you tell if it is a good-quality oil? Generally the price is a good guide. Be prepared to pay for good olive oil. Try to taste before you buy. Good shops will let you do this.

The process of making olive oil is about separating the *sansa* and the *acqua* from the *olio* — the skins and pips and the water from the oil.

It takes five kilograms of olives to produce one litre of oil, so only about four to five bottles come from each tree each season.

Heat is the enemy of olive oil, so the best extra virgin olive oils are cold pressed — extracted from the olives at a temperature less than 27°C. Traditionally, and still very commonly, extra virgin olive oil is pressed using a simple granite millstone and a hydraulic press.

Extra virgin olive oil has a low smoke point, which is the temperature at which it breaks down and begins to burn and smoke. Therefore extra virgin olive oil is never used for deep frying or when a high cooking temperature is required. Usually sunflower oil is used for deep frying in Italy.

Different grades of olive oil are used in the kitchen. The extra virgin olive oil is used for drizzling over cooked foods or for dipping bread. A less piquant olive oil is used for roasting and sautéing and a light olive oil is used for fish or delicate dishes and light dressings.

Once the olive oil bottle has been opened the contents will start to oxidise. It should be stored in a cool, dark place — not as most people do, by the oven. It keeps best in dark green glass bottles or tins to avoid exposure to sunlight.

Every area of Italy thinks its olive oil is the best, the quintessential Italian olive oil, but it is all a matter of personal taste. As with wine, you can detect a whole host of background flavours in the oil and all elements, from the sun, moon and stars, to terroir and sunshine hours will affect the finished product.

Balsamic Vinegar

Balsamic vinegar comes from Modena and the surrounding area of Reggio Emilia. It has its own protective designation. Balsamic vinegar was originally made as a tonic and the word balsamic means 'health-giving'.

Unlike other vinegars, balsamic isn't made from wine but from the must (juice) of the Trebbiano grape, which has been cooked very slowly to concentrate it. The vinegar is aged for at least twelve years in a series of barrels, starting with oak then chestnut, cherry, acacia, juniper, ash and mulberry. The resulting vinegar is thick and syrupy.

There are good vinegars produced all over Italy outside the designated area but these have to be named *condimento balsamico*.

Italian Cheeses

Parmigiano-Reggiano (Parmesan)

This is probably the most famous cheese in the world. European Community laws make it illegal to call a cheese Parmigiano-Reggiano unless it is produced to traditional

specifications within a designated area. There are about 600 cheese manufacturers supplied by 10,000 dairies that are involved in Parmigiano-Reggiano production. The cheese is usually aged for two years.

Grana Padano

A very similar cheese to Parmigiano-Reggiano but made in a different area. It also has its own special identity and EC regulations. The Grana Padano area is much larger than that for Parmigiano-Reggiano, therefore the volume of cheese production is larger and the cheese less expensive. Mamma uses Grana Padano in cooking and saves the Parmigiano-Reggiano for grating at the table. Grana Padano is aged for between nine and eighteen months.

Pecorino

A hard, salted sheep's milk cheese made all over Italy. Different regions have their own specific characteristics and pecorino is sold in varying degrees of ripeness, from young to mature, according to local styles. The mature cheese can be quite sweet and nutty and is delicious served with fruit and honey drizzled over as an appetiser or in lieu of dessert.

Asiago

This is a semi-fat cheese made from cow's milk which has been made since the Middle Ages. There are two varieties. The young cheese — Asiago Pressato — has lots of holes in it and a springy rind. The older cheese — Asiago d'Allevo — is very delicate and tangy.

Fontina

A semi-soft cow's milk cheese made mainly in Northern Italy. It has quite a nutty taste.

PECORINO DA TAVOLA

Brancaleone da Norcia

Ingredienti: Latte di Pecora Pasterizzato,
caglio, sale, fermenti lattici selezionati
Trattato in superficie con conservante E 235

Venduto da: Brancale...
Via Colombo, 12 - 06046 N...
www.brancaleone...orcia.it

Loc. Piano di Grignano Lotto
Manciano

Prodotto da...

Da vendere a peso. Conservare in luogo fresco ed asciutto
Prodotto soggetto a calo peso naturale • Incarto per alimenti

GRANCHE MILLEFIORINI
NORCIA

IT
00016
CE

02 31 14

Gorgonzola

Italy's famous blue cheese. This comes in two styles: Dolce, a sweet, mild-tasting cheese, or Piccante, a matured, stronger-flavoured cheese with marked blue-green veining.

Mozzarella

This can be made from cow's milk but the best comes from the milk of the water buffalo. The process used to make this type of cheese is called *pasta filata* or stretched cheese, in which the curds are cut and stretched. Balls of mozzarella are sold floating in watery whey.

Mascarpone

This is a soft white cream cheese and is the key ingredient in tiramisu.

Provolone

Mostly made with cow's milk, it is a pale yellow, shiny cheese which is often moulded into shapes — cones, balls, animals etc.

Taleggio

The name Taleggio has been used only since the early twentieth century, but this cow's milk cheese dates back to the tenth century. It is a washed-rind cheese — quite mild when young but becoming more tangy as it ages.

Ricotta

The word ricotta means re-cooked. This is technically not a cheese as it is made from whey and cheeses are made from curds. It is similar to cottage cheese in texture and is used in sweet and savoury dishes. It is sometimes smoked, which gives a fabulous, distinctive flavour.

Italian Meats — salumi

No, not salami. *Salumi* is the generic name given to cured meats. The making of salumi was a way of preserving meats before refrigeration and also a way of using up every part of the animal, even the blood.

As with many foods, every Italian region boasts typical local cured meats of extraordinary taste. Good salumi carry a DOP number, which indicates a protected designation of origin — like the classification for Parmigiano-Reggiano cheese.

Salami

Every region has its own special variety of salami. They are made with chopped meat and hard fat, seasoned and spiced, and forced into casings to hang and cure. Some have chillies, peppercorns and garlic added. They are usually sold finely sliced to order, wrapped in greaseproof paper. Best eaten on the day of slicing.

Prosciutto crudo

The word *prosciutto* simply means ham. *Crudo* means raw. These hams are salted and dried rather than cooked. Parma ham and prosciutto are one and the same. Different areas guard the making of their special hams religiously. They are all made in a similar way and air dried but the breed of pig and its diet, together with sunshine hours, air temperature, soil type etc, all influence the finished product.

Pancetta

This is cured belly pork or streaky bacon. It can be smoked, flat or rolled into rounds. Most is sold sliced to order. *Pancetta coppata* is made from the back of the neck of the pig and is usually less fatty than regular pancetta.

Speck

This is smoked prosciutto and is traditional to the Alto Adige region of Italy.

Mortadella

A cooked spiced pork, specific to Bologna.

Bresaola

A raw boar meat, marinated in wine and spices before curing.

Guanciale

This is the cured cheek of a pig and is an essential ingredient in several dishes, including the Roman-style carbonara and amatriciana sauces.

Sopressata

Every part of a pig's head is used for this — tongue, ears, the lot. It is cooked with spices and lemon and pressed into a casing.

Coppa

Back-of-the-neck pork, cured and air dried in a sausage casing.

ROMA 163
MACERATA 96
SPOLETO 48
CASCIA 12
PERUGIA 91
OCCAPORENA 17
TERNI 61
ONTELEONE 35
FOLIGNO 59
EONESSA 37
TRIPONZO 11

First Tastes, Antipasto & Appetisers

I make these in batch-lots on trays baked in the oven but they can also be made in a non-stick frypan or on a silicone sheet on a barbecue plate. A really delicious and easy crispy snack.

Frico — Parmesan Crackers with Fennel & Cumin Seeds

Makes 16–20

2 cups finely shaved or grated parmesan
2 tablespoons cumin seeds
2 tablespoons fennel seeds

Preheat the oven to 180°C. Cover 2 large oven trays with non-stick baking paper or silicone sheets.

Combine the grated cheese and seeds, then sprinkle little piles of the mixture in 5 cm circles on the prepared trays, with at least 5 cm between each pile.

Bake until the cheese bubbles and starts to crisp — about 4–5 minutes. Do not let them go too brown — the cheese should just be melted together and bubbly.

Cool for 1 minute, then lift off the tray with a spatula and cool completely on a wire rack. When still hot they can be draped over a rolling pin or bottle to set in a curved shape if desired.

When completely cool, store in an airtight container.

Serve with drinks.

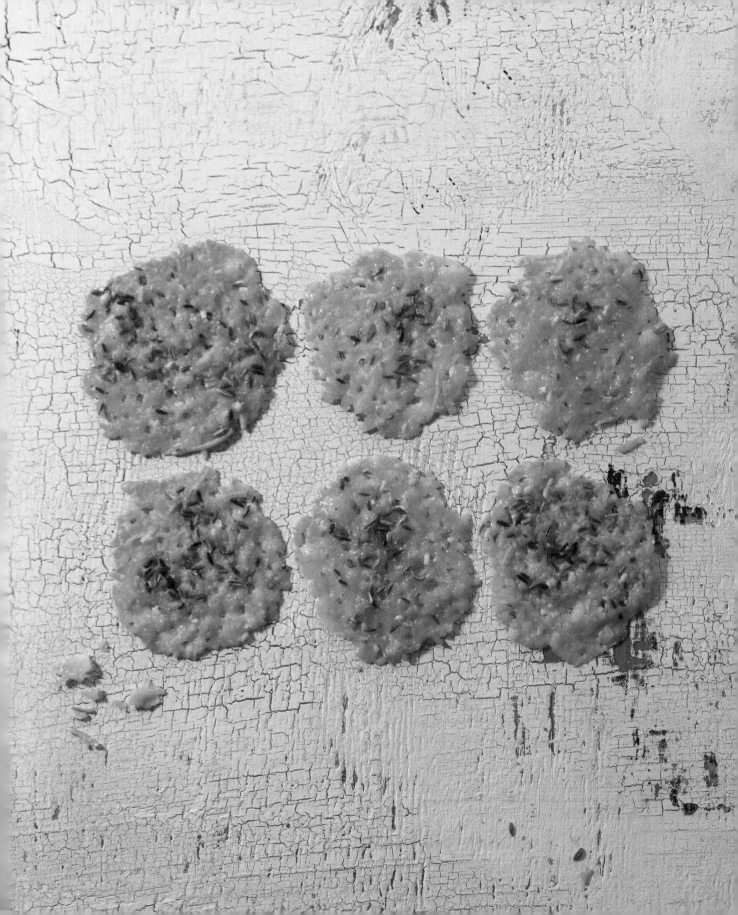

A very simple idea of Mamma's for a delicious appetiser.
She would serve these with some slices of focaccia or ciabatta.

Pear with Pecorino & Honey

Serves 6

3 pears, ripe but firm

1 cup coarsely shaved pecorino

6 thyme sprigs

2 handfuls baby rocket leaves

1 tablespoon honey (we used a lovely floral one, from hives near lavender fields)

Heat the pizza oven or grill to high heat.

Slice the pears lengthways into 4–5 slices. Lay the slices flat on a pizza paddle or roasting dish.

Sprinkle the shaved pecorino over the pear slices, then pull the leaves off the thyme sprigs and sprinkle over the cheese. Place in the oven or under the grill for a few minutes until the cheese bubbles and browns. Remove from the heat and transfer to serving plates. Add a few rocket leaves and drizzle with the honey. Eat immediately.

Black Olive Tapenade

Makes 1½ cups

2 cups pitted black olives
6–8 anchovy fillets packed in oil
2 tablespoons capers, rinsed and drained
2 cloves garlic, peeled
grated rind and juice of 1 lemon
¼ cup extra virgin olive oil
salt and freshly ground black pepper

Whiz together all the ingredients except the salt and pepper in a food processor, scraping down the sides of the bowl a couple of times. Process until the mixture is smoothly combined. Season with salt and black pepper.

Serve with chunks of crusty bread or as a spread for crostini.

This will keep in a small, covered container or jar in the fridge for up to a month.

Crostini are a useful way of using up day-old bread.
They are made from baguettes or bread sticks.

Crostini with Gorgonzola & Black Olive Tapenade

Preheat the oven to 180°C.

Slice the bread into rounds about ½ cm thick. Brush with olive oil. I use extra virgin olive oil for its great flavour and colour.

Place on an oven tray and sprinkle with flaky sea salt or garlic salt. Bake in a single layer for 15–20 minutes, until golden brown, crispy and dry. Cool on a wire rack.

All kinds of toppings can be used but I particularly love crostini spread with black olive tapenade (see page 38) and a little slice of Gorgonzola, served just warmed to melt the cheese.

These can be made with large whole olives or with stuffed olives. At the cook school we eat beautiful big olives, stuffed with anchovies, which are delicious.

Fried Crumbed Olives

Makes 24

24 large green olives, whole, pitted or
  stuffed as desired
½ cup flour
2 eggs, lightly beaten together
1½ cups dry breadcrumbs
oil for deep frying

Dry the olives on paper towels, then roll them in the flour before dipping them in the egg and coating in breadcrumbs. Repeat the egg and breadcrumbs so the olives have 2 layers of the coating.

Chill in the fridge for an hour before deep frying.

Heat the oil in a deep fryer to approximately 190°C.

Cook until golden and crispy — about 2 minutes. Drain on paper towels before serving warm.

Bruschetta con Mozzarella e Pomodoro

4 slices rustic country bread (focaccia
   or ciabatta)
2 garlic cloves, cut in half
4 tablespoons olive oil
150 g buffalo mozzarella, sliced
2 ripe tomatoes, sliced
salt and freshly ground black pepper
basil leaves to garnish

Preheat the oven grill to high.

Grill the bread on both sides. Rub the cut garlic over the toasted bread to infuse it with flavour. Drizzle the bread with olive oil and top with the sliced mozzarella and tomatoes, then add another drizzle of oil, and season with salt and pepper.

Garnish with a basil leaf or two if desired.

These are very simple little snacks which I've successfully made on a barbecue plate, but they can also be made in a non-stick frypan. Wonderful to serve with drinks.

Salami & Fennel Seed Wafers

Makes 15

½ cup grated parmesan
1–2 tablespoons fennel seeds
30 slices thinly cut salami

Mix the grated parmesan and fennel seeds together. Sandwich this mixture between 2 slices of salami, and repeat until all the mixture is used up. Fry in a non-stick pan or grill on a barbecue plate for about 1 minute each side over medium-high heat. Serve warm.

These are glorified little toasted sandwiches. Very moreish.
Add a salad and you have lunch, or they can be served with drinks.

Fried Anchovy & Garlic Mozzarella Sandwiches

1 garlic bulb
4 anchovy fillets
1 bunch Italian parsley
12 thin slices ciabatta or baguette
250 g buffalo mozzarella, thinly sliced
oil for frying

Preheat the oven to 200°C.

Wrap the bulb of garlic in tinfoil and roast for 15–20 minutes until the garlic is very soft. Cut off the top of the bulb and squeeze out all the cloves.

In a food processor, whiz the roasted garlic, anchovies and parsley to a paste. Spread on all the slices of ciabatta, then sandwich pairs of them together with slices of mozzarella. Fry until golden brown on both sides — about 1 minute each side. Drain on a paper towel and serve hot.

A very simple idea but an item you will see on every menu in Italy.

Melon & Fresh Figs Wrapped in Prosciutto

Simply wrap a fine rasher of prosciutto around a peeled melon slice or fresh ripe fig and garnish with fresh mint if desired.

Serve nice and chilled.

These little baby peppers taste like capsicums and are sweet and delicious. Fat chilli peppers could be substituted if you can cope with the fiery blast. I've grown these little peppers successfully from seeds bought at a local garden centre and they are also available in the fresh vegetable department of good supermarkets. They come in three colours — red, yellow and orange. Allow two peppers per serving as an appetiser.

Piccolo Peppers Stuffed with Bocconcini & Wrapped in Bacon

Preheat the oven to 200°C.

Slice the peppers in half lengthways, leaving a little stalk. Scoop out any seeds and membranes.

Place a small piece of bocconcini in the cavity of each pepper, and wrap in a rasher of streaky bacon. Lie flat on an oven tray and bake for 12–15 minutes until the bacon is crisp.

Serve warm.

For every zucchini that grows there are actually two flowers on the plant. The male flower has no fruit, and the female flower is attached to the zucchini itself. Both flowers can be stuffed and fried, but the male ones have long spiky stalks which make them easier to dip into the oil.

Stuffed Zucchini Flowers

Serves 4

8 zucchini flowers
oil for deep frying

For the stuffing
½ cup fresh ricotta
½ cup finely chopped mozzarella
¼ cup finely grated parmesan
grated rind of 1 lemon
salt and freshly ground black pepper

For the batter
1 egg
100 ml milk
¾ cup flour
60 ml sparkling mineral water
pinch salt
pinch caster sugar

Gently open out the flowers, remove the stamens and check for any little insects.

Mix all the stuffing ingredients together in a bowl and carefully spoon the stuffing into the opened flower heads. Twist the petals to close over the filling.

To make the batter, beat the egg with the milk using a wire whisk or hand-held electric beater. Slowly add the flour, whisking it to combine. Add the sparkling water, salt and sugar and combine.

Heat the oil in a deep fryer to 175°C.

Dip the flowers into the batter, shaking off any excess. Fry for about 3 minutes until crispy golden brown. Cook just a few at a time. Drain on paper towels and serve warm.

As an alternative, the flowers can be filled with the cheese mixture and perhaps a slice of prosciutto, then sprinkled with breadcrumbs and baked in a hot oven for about 15 minutes at 200°C until the crumbs are toasted golden.

Smaller or First Courses & Soups

Fava (broad) beans are a staple food on the Italian table in spring and are wonderful paired with the season's new mint leaves.

Fava Beans with Mint, Garlic & Prosciutto

Makes 6

2 kg fresh fava beans in the pod (to make
    approximately 3 cups of peeled beans)
3 tablespoons extra virgin olive oil
2 slices prosciutto, snipped into
    small pieces
2 cloves garlic, crushed
salt and freshly ground black pepper
1 teaspoon balsamic vinegar
handful young spring mint leaves

Peel the beans and plunge them into boiling water for 3 minutes — 4 minutes if they are older and larger. Drain and transfer to a bowl of cold water. Soak for a few minutes, then pop the beans out of their grey skins, releasing the bright green inner bean. (Frozen broad beans work equally well for this dish. If using frozen beans defrost and peel. They won't need any further cooking.)

Place the oil in a frypan over medium-high heat and when hot, add the chopped prosciutto. Sauté for 1 minute, then add the garlic. Cool for 30 seconds before adding the drained beans. Toss to warm through. Season with salt and pepper, add the vinegar and fresh mint leaves. Check the seasoning and serve warm.

Mamma's Special Tomatoes Stuffed with Basil, White Wine & Rice

Makes 6

6 large, ripe, bright red, vine-ripened
  tomatoes
2 tablespoons olive oil
½ cup Arborio rice
1 clove garlic, peeled
good pinch flaky sea salt and freshly
  ground black pepper
handful fresh basil leaves
1 cup white wine, or water

Preheat the oven to 150°C.

Turn tomatoes upside down and slice the bottom of each most of the way through so that a flap about the size of a soft-drink bottle top is formed. Squeeze the flesh of each tomato into a sieve over a small bowl, being careful not to split the skin. Squish the pulp and seeds into the sieve using the back of a spoon and reserve the juice. Discard the pulp.

Heat the oil in a large frypan and add the rice and garlic. Cook for 2 minutes, stirring to coat each grain of rice in oil. Remove the garlic. Add the strained tomato liquid and season with salt and pepper. Tear the basil into the mixture, then remove the pan from the heat.

Divide the mixture between the tomato shells and place the stuffed tomatoes in a shallow roasting dish. Top up each with white wine or water. Close the lids and bake for approximately 1 hour until the rice has swelled and filled the tomato with risotto. You may need to top up the tomatoes with extra wine during cooking as the rice absorbs the liquid.

Serve as a side dish or with a few rocket leaves as a vegetable course. Perfect with crusty bread for lunch.

Rocket Frittata

Serves 8–10 as an appetiser

2 handfuls baby rocket leaves
   (about 60 g), trimmed and roughly
   chopped

2 handfuls baby spinach leaves, trimmed
   and roughly chopped

1 small leek, finely sliced

2 cloves garlic, crushed

50 ml olive oil

6 eggs

salt and freshly ground black pepper

grated rind and juice of 1 lemon

½ cup fresh ricotta (about 100 g)

½ cup finely grated pecorino, plus
   extra to garnish

Mamma uses a steamer but I prefer to microwave the rocket, spinach and leek for 1 minute. Place the vegetables in a colander and squeeze out all excess liquid.

Preheat the oven grill to high.

Place the crushed garlic and olive oil in a medium-sized (16–18 cm) frypan and heat over medium-high heat. Whisk the eggs and season with salt and pepper. Add the grated lemon rind and juice. Pour into the frypan. Add the chopped vegetables, crumble over the ricotta and sprinkle over the pecorino.

Cook until the base is firmly set and browned nicely — about 3–4 minutes — then place the pan under the grill for a further 2–3 minutes to brown and set the surface. Cut into wedges and garnish with a shaving of pecorino.

There are lots of versions of this soup, but this is the one Mamma taught me.

Country-style White Bean Soup

Serves 4–6

4 tablespoons extra virgin olive oil
1 onion, roughly chopped
2 leeks, sliced
1 large floury potato, peeled and chopped
4 cloves garlic, crushed
6 cups chicken or vegetable stock
400 g can cannellini beans, drained
 (reserve the liquid)
2 cups shredded savoy cabbage
½ cup chopped Italian parsley
2 tablespoons chopped fresh oregano
flaky sea salt and freshly ground black
 pepper
shaved parmesan to serve

Heat the olive oil in a large saucepan and cook the onion, leeks, potato and garlic for 3–4 minutes, stirring. Add the stock and the liquid from the beans. Cover the saucepan and allow to simmer for 15–20 minutes.

Stir in the cabbage, beans and herbs. Season generously with salt and pepper and cook for a further 5 minutes. Tip half of the soup into a blender or food processor and purée. Return this to the remaining soup. Check the seasoning and reheat. Serve with shavings of parmesan and fresh bread.

Pappa al Pomodoro
(Fresh Tomato & Bread Soup)

Serves 4

100 ml olive oil
1 onion, finely diced
5 cloves garlic, crushed
12 large ripe tomatoes, or 2 x 400 g
  cans peeled tomatoes
250 ml chicken stock
1 teaspoon red wine vinegar
2 teaspoons dried oregano
salt and freshly ground black pepper
½ loaf day-old ciabatta or similar bread,
  torn into bite-sized pieces
extra virgin olive oil
basil leaves to garnish

Place the olive oil, onion and garlic in a medium-sized saucepan and sauté for 6–7 minutes until the onion is translucent.

Meanwhile, boil a kettle. Place the tomatoes, with the skins scored, in a large bowl. Pour over the boiling water and cover and stand for 3–4 minutes until the skins split. Drain and, when cool enough to handle, peel the tomatoes and coarsely chop.

Add the chopped tomatoes to the onion and garlic and then pour in the chicken stock. Bring to the boil. Add the vinegar and oregano and season well with salt and pepper. Simmer for 20 minutes, checking the seasoning.

Place the torn bread into four bowls and ladle the soup over the bread. Drizzle each bowl with extra virgin olive oil, scatter with fresh basil leaves and add another good grind of pepper.

This is wonderful served as a separate, smaller vegetable course or as a lunch, with crusty bread.

Roasted Green Beans with Pinenuts, Lemon & Parmesan

Serves 4–6

2 handfuls (600 g) green beans, topped and tailed
4 cloves garlic, crushed
¼ cup extra virgin olive oil
grated rind and juice of 2 lemons
salt and freshly ground black pepper
¼ cup pinenuts
¼ cup grated parmesan
handful Italian parsley, chopped

Preheat the oven to 200°C.

Toss the beans, garlic, olive oil, lemon rind and juice together with a generous pinch of salt and pepper. Mix to coat the beans well.

Spread in a large roasting dish and cook for around 20 minutes, stirring a couple of times. Scatter over the pinenuts during the last few minutes of cooking, then transfer the beans to a serving plate. Sprinkle with parmesan and parsley, adding another good grind of pepper. Serve warm or at room temperature.

This is a very thin fritatta — only the thickness of one slice of potato. The truffle flavour is quite intense so just serve a small portion.

Potato Truffle Frittata

Serves 4

2 large, waxy new-season potatoes, unpeeled

4 eggs

100 ml cream

handful Italian parsley, chopped

flaky sea salt and freshly ground black pepper

30 g butter

1 teaspoon truffle oil, or a small truffle, shaved

¼ cup shaved parmesan

Boil the potatoes until cooked. Drain and, when cool enough to handle, peel off the skins and slice into 2–3 mm slices.

Mix together the eggs, cream, parsley, and salt and pepper in a bowl.

Preheat the oven grill to high.

Heat a 30 cm non-stick frypan and melt the butter. Swirl the butter around to coat the surface of the frypan. Pour in the egg mixture and layer with the sliced potato. Do not stir. Drizzle the surface with the truffle oil, or sprinkle over the shaved truffle. Scatter over the parmesan.

Cook until the base is firmly set and browned nicely — about 3–4 minutes — then place the pan under the grill for a further 2–3 minutes to brown and set the surface.

This is a delicious, smaller, nibbling kind of dish. You need to use a firm, block-style ricotta cheese — sheep's ricotta if possible. Softer ricottas are not the right texture for this dish.

Baked Ricotta with Sundried Tomato & Basil Pesto

Serves 6

600 g fresh ricotta
1 tablespoon chopped Italian parsley
1 tablespoon chopped basil
1 tablespoon chopped marjoram
1 tablespoon chopped thyme leaves
salt and freshly ground black pepper
1 cup sundried tomatoes in olive oil
1 cup pitted black olives
1 cup pistachio nuts, or walnuts
handful basil leaves
10 ripe plum tomatoes, peeled, deseeded
   and chopped
6 slices rustic country-style bread
   (focaccia or ciabatta), toasted
6 sprigs basil to garnish
extra virgin olive oil to serve

Preheat the oven to 200°C. Spray 6 small ramekins or dariole moulds with non-stick baking spray.

Mix the ricotta and fresh herbs together. Season with salt and pepper. Spoon into the prepared moulds. Bake for 12–15 minutes.

Place the sundried tomatoes, olives, nuts and basil leaves in a food processor and mix to a chunky pesto.

Season the chopped tomatoes with salt and pepper.

To serve, place the toast slices on 6 plates. Turn out a baked ricotta onto each piece of toast, then spoon over the pesto. Divide the tomatoes between the 6 portions and garnish with basil sprigs. Drizzle with olive oil to serve.

The essence of Italian cooking is simplicity. The key is to concentrate on just a few flavours.

Salads & Vegetables

We identify with Italian cuisine.
Essentially it's food born of poverty,
resourcefulness and frugality, descending
from a rural past.

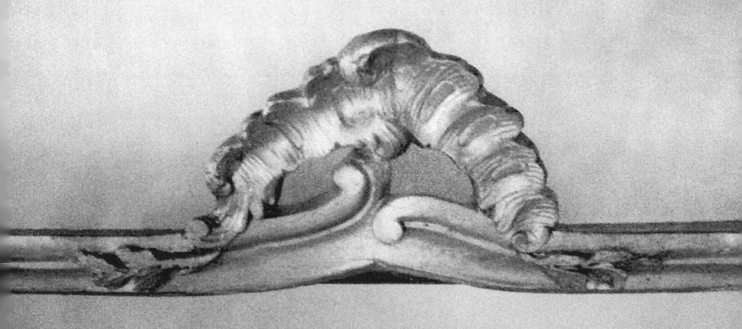

So simple, so delicious.

Mozzarella, Tomato, Fresh Basil & Caper Salad

Serves 4

2 large, bright red, vine-ripened tomatoes
200 g buffalo mozzarella
8–10 basil leaves
¼ cup capers, either salted
  or brined, rinsed and drained
4 tablespoons extra virgin olive oil
salt and freshly ground black pepper

Cut the tomatoes and mozzarella into 8 slices.

Arrange the slices with the basil on a serving plate — tomato, mozzarella, basil, tomato, mozzarella, basil etc. Sprinkle over the capers and drizzle over the olive oil. Season to taste with salt and pepper.

Sunflower Salad

Serves 4–6 as a side dish

1 large organic (unsprayed) sunflower
4 handfuls fresh baby salad leaves
2 cups sliced white button mushrooms
¼ cup sunflower seeds
¼ cup olive or sunflower oil
1 tablespoon white vinegar
salt and freshly ground black pepper

Pull off the bright yellow petals of the sunflower and place in a bowl with the washed salad leaves. Add the mushroom slices and sunflower seeds.

Mix together the oil and vinegar and season with salt and pepper. Drizzle the dressing over the salad and toss to mix well. Serve immediately.

Oven-roasted Asparagus with Fried Capers

Serves 4

500 g fresh asparagus, preferably thin,
even-sized spears

3 tablespoons extra virgin olive oil

3 tablespoons capers, rinsed and dried on
paper towels

1 tablespoon balsamic vinegar

2 tablespoons shaved parmesan to garnish

Preheat the oven to 200°C.

Trim the ends of the asparagus and place the spears on a baking tray or in a roasting dish. Drizzle with 1 tablespoon of olive oil and roast for 12–15 minutes.

Meanwhile, heat 1 tablespoon of olive oil in a small frypan and fry the capers until crisp. Drain on paper towels.

Remove the asparagus from the oven. Place on a serving dish. Drizzle over the vinegar and the remaining tablespoon of olive oil. Sprinkle over the capers and parmesan.

Fennel, Celery & Blood Orange Salad with Honey Mustard Dressing

Serves 6

3 fennel bulbs
1 celery heart
4 blood oranges
2 tablespoons grainy mustard
3 tablespoons extra virgin olive oil
2 tablespoons honey
juice of 1 lemon
½ cup roughly chopped Italian parsley
salt and freshly ground black pepper

Finely shave the fennel and celery heart with a mandolin and place in iced water. Grate off and reserve the rind of the oranges, then peel and slice the flesh. Discard any pips.

In a small bowl, whisk together the grainy mustard with the olive oil, honey, lemon juice and orange rind.

Drain the fennel and celery and mix with the oranges. Drizzle over the honey mustard dressing and garnish with the parsley. Season with salt and pepper.

Aubergine Involtini

Serves 6

4 red capsicums
¾ cup olive oil
1 aubergine (approximately 350 g)
salt and freshly ground black pepper
½ cup prepared pesto
200 g soft goat's cheese
basil sprigs to garnish

Preheat the oven to 200°C.

Place the capsicums on a baking tray and drizzle with ¼ cup of the olive oil. Roast until the skins start to colour and wrinkle — about 30 minutes. Remove from the heat and cover with tinfoil. When cool enough to handle, peel off the skins, slice into quarters and remove the stalks and seeds.

Slice the aubergine lengthways into 5 mm slices. Brush with the remaining ½ cup of oil. The aubergine will soak up the oil. Season well with salt and pepper and roast for 12–15 minutes until the aubergine slices are tender but still hold their shape nicely. Cool.

Spread the pesto on the slices of aubergine. Top with the pieces of capsicum, then spread with the goat's cheese. Season well and roll up firmly from the pointy (stem) end of the aubergine. Slice and place on a platter seam-side down. Garnish with sprigs of basil if desired. Serve at room temperature.

Zucchini & Capsicums — Mamma's Style

Serves 6

6 medium zucchini

3 red capsicums

3 yellow capsicums

300 g minced meat (pork, beef or lamb)

1 egg

1 cup fresh white breadcrumbs

½ cup finely grated parmesan

1 tablespoon chopped fresh oregano,
   or 1 teaspoon dried oregano

1 teaspoon dried thyme

6 fresh basil leaves, chopped

1 clove garlic, crushed

salt and freshly ground black pepper

1 tablespoon chopped Italian parsley,
   to garnish

Preheat the oven to 180°C.

Using a long vegetable corer, like an apple corer, scoop out a tunnel through the middle of each zucchini. Cut the capsicums in half and remove the seeds and ribs.

Thoroughly mix the mince, egg, breadcrumbs, parmesan, herbs, garlic and generous amounts of salt and pepper. Using your fingers, push a long sausage of the mince mixture, from both ends, into each hollowed-out zucchini.

If the capsicums will not sit flat, slice a piece off the bottom. Use the piece you've sliced off to patch the inside of the capsicum, covering the hole you have made. Spoon the remaining mixture into the halved capsicums.

Place the vegetables in a large roasting dish and bake for 25–30 minutes until the meat is cooked through.

Garnish with parsley and serve warm.

The peppery rocket really marries well with the texture and flavour of the melons.

Melon & Rocket Salad

Serves 4

1 small rockmelon, deseeded
½ watermelon, roughly the size of the rockmelon, deseeded
4 handfuls baby rocket leaves
¼ cup extra virgin olive oil
2 tablespoons white wine vinegar
salt and freshly ground black pepper

Using a melon baller, scoop out the flesh of the melons. Put the melon balls in a large bowl with the baby rocket.

Whisk together the olive oil, vinegar, salt and pepper. Drizzle over the salad and toss to coat the melon in the dressing. Serve immediately.

You don't eat the bay leaves but their lovely flavour is imparted to the potatoes, and they make a great garnish.

New Potatoes Squashed with Fresh Bay Leaves & Lemon

Serves 6 as a side dish

36 small new-season potatoes (Jersey
 Bennes are good), scrubbed
3–4 small branches bay leaves
grated rind and juice of 2 lemons
¼ cup extra virgin olive oil
flaky sea salt and freshly ground black
 pepper

Preheat the oven to 200°C.

Boil the potatoes in their skins until just tender — about 15–18 minutes. Drain and cool so that they can be easily handled.

Place the bay branches in a roasting tray and squash or flatten the potatoes into the bay leaves. Press them down so their skins split and they squish open.

Whisk together the lemon rind and juice with the olive oil and drizzle over the squashed potatoes. Sprinkle generously with salt and pepper. Roast for 30–40 minutes until the leaves are scorched and the potatoes crispy and golden brown. Discard the bay leaves to serve or use them as a garnish on the serving dish.

Patate al Forno (Rosemary, Sea Salt & Sage Roasted Potatoes)

Serves 6 as a side dish

- 1.5 kg potatoes, well-scrubbed and cut into wedges or quarters
- 2 x 10 cm branches rosemary
- 20 sage leaves
- 100 ml olive oil
- flaky sea salt
- 1 bulb garlic, broken into cloves but unpeeled

Preheat the oven to 200°C.

Place the potato wedges in a roasting tray. Strip the leaves off the rosemary branches and scatter the leaves over the potatoes. Sprinkle over the sage leaves, olive oil, sea salt and garlic cloves. Don't be mean with the salt! Stir the potatoes to coat evenly in the oil.

Roast for 30–40 minutes until nicely crispy, golden and cooked through.

Finocchi Gratinati (Baked Fennel Gratin)

Serves 4–6

3–4 fennel bulbs (about 750 g)
1¼ cups full-cream milk
25 g butter
1 tablespoon flour
salt and freshly ground black pepper
½ cup dry white breadcrumbs
½ cup grated parmesan

Preheat oven to 220°C. Spray a small pie or lasagne dish with non-stick baking spray.

Chop off the root ends and stalks of the fennel. Cut the bulb into quarters or thick slices. Place in a large sauté pan or saucepan and pour over the milk. Simmer for 10–15 minutes to soften the fennel. Strain, reserving the milk. Lay the fennel in the prepared dish.

In a small saucepan, melt the butter, then whisk in the flour. Season with salt and pepper. While whisking over medium heat, add the reserved milk. Stir until the sauce thickens. Check the seasoning — be generous with the salt and pepper.

Pour the sauce over the fennel. Sprinkle with the breadcrumbs and parmesan. Bake for 20–25 minutes until nicely browned.

Sautéed Fresh Porcini & Garlic

Serves 4

500 g fresh porcini mushrooms
½ cup olive oil
25 g butter
6 small shallots, finely chopped
1 teaspoon lemon juice
flaky sea salt and freshly ground black
   pepper
handful Italian parsley, chopped

Wipe the porcini clean with a soft tea towel. Remove the stems. Slice the caps and chop the stems into small dice.

Heat the olive oil in a large frypan. (It might seem like a lot of oil but you need it to get the porcini properly browned. You will pour off the excess.) When the oil is good and hot, fry the porcini cap slices until quite brown and starting to crisp. Remove the mushrooms with a slotted spoon and drain on paper towels.

Carefully tip most of the oil from the pan, leaving about 1 tablespoon. Return the pan to the heat and add the butter, shallots and diced porcini stems. Sauté for 2–3 minutes. Add the cooked porcini slices, lemon juice, salt and pepper and parsley. Serve immediately with crusty bread.

Artichokes

Artichokes have been a key food in Italy since they were first cultivated in Etruscan times. They were popular not only for their delicate, slightly bitter taste, but because they were an important medicinal vegetable, used to stimulate and protect the liver and gallbladder. They were also used to treat digestive disorders.

Artichokes are an edible thistle but can quickly go from delicately tender to tough and prickly if harvested too late. Young, tightly closed globe artichokes are the ones to go for.

Trim and shorten the stalks to about 5–6 cm long and peel off the outer covering of the stalks. Remove the first, tough outer leaves and the dry prickly thorns on the remaining leaves. I usually just cut off the top quarter of the artichoke head.

Add a squeeze of lemon juice to a pot of cold water and plunge in the trimmed artichokes. Bring the water to the boil and simmer for 30–40 minutes. Remove the artichokes and drain upside down for a moment or two to remove excess water. Serve with a bowl of simple dressing such as melted butter or hollandaise sauce on the side.

To eat, pull off a leaf, dip the base into the sauce, put the leaf in your mouth and pull out between your teeth to scrape off the flesh. The first leaves have hardly any edible flesh but as you get nearer the choke or centre, the leaves get more and more tender. Scoop the hairy part in the centre out with a teaspoon and discard, then eat the best part — the base and stem of the artichoke.

It's a messy business! There is lots of debris, so offer your guests a bowl to toss the outer leaves and discarded bits into. This is a fun, sociable way to share these beautiful vegetables.

Because the crop doesn't all come to maturity at the same time, Mamma picks the artichokes as they ripen and boils them up daily. Then, when cooked, she slices them in half, discarding the tough outer leaves, and places them in a large jar, covering them in olive oil. She adds to the jar until it is full, dunking the artichokes down below the surface, making sure they are well covered in oil. The artichokes can be used as desired and the oil in dressings etc. They will keep for six to eight weeks. I store mine in the fridge but Mamma keeps hers in the pantry. When stored in the fridge they need to be brought to room temperature before serving.

This is an easy salad using canned or preserved artichoke hearts. It is great served with good bread as part of a shared meal.

Artichoke & Lemon Salad

Serves 4 as a side dish

400 g artichoke hearts, from a can or jar
2 cloves garlic, crushed
grated rind and juice of 2 lemons
¼ cup extra virgin olive oil
handful Italian parsley, chopped
flaky sea salt and freshly ground black
  pepper

Drain the artichokes and chop into quarters. Mix with all the other ingredients, seasoning well. Allow the flavours to develop for a couple of hours, or overnight, before serving.

Gnocchi, Risotto & Polenta

To Make Potato Gnocchi

Serves 4–6

1 kg potatoes — use a very floury and starchy variety such as Agria or Desiree
salt
2 eggs
1¼ cups 00 or high-grade flour

Scrub the potatoes and leave whole in their skins. Place in a saucepan, cover with cold water and bring to the boil. Cook until tender when pierced with a sharp knife — about 25–30 minutes.

Drain the potatoes in a colander and as soon as they are cool enough to handle, but still hot, peel off and discard the skins. Press the warm potatoes through a potato ricer. The ricer will keep the mash fluffy and aerated. If you do not have a potato ricer, force the potato through a sieve.

Place the potato in a large bowl or in a mound on the bench and add a few pinches of salt. Mix in the eggs and three-quarters of the flour with your hands, combining into a dough. Add extra flour only as you need it. This is important — you do not want to add more than is necessary to make a soft dough. The eggs help the dough to stay together and firm up when it is cooked.

Dust your work surface with flour and flatten the dough down into a plate shape, about 2 cm thick. Cut into 2 cm wide strips. Roll each strip into a long sausage shape then cut into 1.5 cm pieces.

Mamma never shapes her gnocchi any further, but other people use a fork or a gnocchi paddle (like a butter pat) to make distinctive little lines on their gnocchi. I think they should look quite home-made, so rough to me looks quite rustic. The important thing is that they are uniform in size so they cook evenly.

It is good to rest the gnocchi at this stage for about an hour before cooking. Mamma doesn't approve of freezing — it's fresh every time for her — but I've successfully frozen gnocchi at this stage and cooked them straight from frozen.

When you're ready to cook the gnocchi, bring a large saucepan of water to the boil. Add 2 tablespoons of sea salt. The salt makes the water very buoyant so it boils with a tumbling motion — it should taste like the sea. Drop the gnocchi into the water all at once, and stir to prevent them sticking together. As soon as they rise to the surface, which should only take a couple of minutes, lift them out with a slotted spoon or drain into a colander and add immediately to your sauce (see following pages).

Important tips

- Have all the ingredients and utensils ready before starting as it is very important to work the gnocchi dough while the potato is still hot.

- Boil the potatoes in their skins so they don't become waterlogged.

- Use older, floury, starchy potatoes for gnocchi, the same as you would for mashed potatoes.

- Only use as much flour as required to form a silky soft dough. Do not overmix and do not use too much flour, as this will make them rubbery. They should melt in the mouth.

- To make gnocchi taste of potato and not flour, it is very important to keep the mixture as dry as possible without the risk of it falling apart . . . there is a fine line!

- As it cooks, the protein in the egg helps the gnocchi keep its shape.

Olive Gnocchi Variation

Add ½ cup of pitted, chopped black
olives to the dough before you roll it
into a sausage shape.

This sauce is totally decadent, but so worth it for a special treat. I have had great success substituting the Gorgonzola with other creamy blue cheeses such as Blue Castello.

Gnocchi with Creamy Gorgonzola Sauce

Makes 4–6 serves

500 ml cream
300 g Gorgonzola Dolce (soft Gorgonzola)
freshly ground black pepper
1 tablespoon flour
1 portion gnocchi (see page 124)

Bring the cream to the boil in a large frypan. Trim any hard rind off the cheese and chop into small dice.

When the cream is boiling, reduce the heat to a gentle simmer. Add the Gorgonzola, reserving a little for the garnish, and a good grind of pepper. Stir until the cheese melts. Whisk in the flour, stirring the sauce until it thickens slightly. Keep warm.

Have warmed bowls at the ready — Mamma says this is very important.

Cook the gnocchi (see page 124). As soon as it is ready, remove from the water with a slotted spoon or drain in a colander. Discard the water and return the drained gnocchi to the hot saucepan. Pour over the sauce. Divide among the bowls and crumble over the reserved Gorgonzola.

Gnocchi with Garlic, Brown Mushrooms & Parsley Sauce

Makes 4–6 serves

2 tablespoons olive oil
50 g butter
4 garlic cloves, thinly sliced
20 brown mushrooms, thinly sliced
   (about 2 cups sliced mushrooms)
1 portion gnocchi (see page 124)
handful Italian parsley, chopped
salt and freshly ground black pepper

Heat a large frypan over medium-high heat. Add the olive oil and butter.

When sizzling, add the sliced garlic and mushrooms. Meanwhile cook the gnocchi. Stir-fry the sauce for 2–3 minutes, then add the strained gnocchi and parsley, and season with salt and pepper. Toss to mix well and coat the gnocchi with the butter. Serve immediately.

At the heart of Italian cookery, no matter how rich or poor you are, is the spirit of conviviality; the pleasure that comes from breaking bread together and sharing a meal with friends.

Risotto

In Italy, risotto tends to be a much more simple affair than the sophisticated recipes you find in restaurants elsewhere. Often it is simply flavoured with saffron or made plainly with onion and garlic with lots of parmesan stirred in at the end.

Every Italian has a strong view on risotto and what a perfect risotto should be like. Some make theirs so the grains of rice have a slight crunch, others prefer very soft and soupy. They are all correct and you just make it how it tastes best to you.

The origins of rice-growing in Italy go back to the days of the Crusaders who returned from the East, bringing back rice and exotic spices. By the fifteenth century rice was commonly grown in northern Italy.

Today the most popular three varieties of rice used for risotto are:

Vialone Nano

Carnaroli

Arborio

Risotto rice is different from any other rice in that the grains have two shells or layers. The outer shell is soft and fragile and the inner coating harder and more robust. It is the relationship between the starches in these two shells and the way in which they break down and absorb the cooking liquid that makes each variety slightly different.

To make a basic risotto

The general rule of thumb is:

500 ml of stock for 100 g of uncooked rice
allow 100 g of uncooked rice per serving

Risotto is only as good as the stock you make it with. A good-flavoured home-made stock is preferable. You begin with a saucepan of hot simmering stock and the *soffritto* — a mixture of finely chopped onion and garlic sautéed in olive oil or butter. A pinch of salt helps the onion to soften without browning.

Next you proceed to the *tostatura* phase — the toasting of the rice. Rice is added to the soffritto and every grain is coated in the buttery or oily onion mixture as it warms. Stir in a glass of wine and allow it to be completely absorbed before adding the stock.

When you toast the grains at the beginning of the cooking process and stir them with the sautéed onion, it warms them up and loosens the outer shell, which releases most of its starch. This is why stirring is important — it breaks down the rice and achieves that lovely creaminess which is so desirable.

Slowly, one ladle at a time, add the hot stock, allowing the starch around the grains to dissolve. Make sure the stock is nearly all absorbed before you add the next ladle, then continue stirring. The whole process takes about 25–30 minutes.

Any delicate ingredients such as seafood or leafy herbs are added right at the end of cooking to protect their fragile texture. More hardy ingredients such as mushrooms can be added earlier for the flavour to blend with the rice.

When the rice is the 'perfect' texture, remove the pan from the heat and cool for a minute before adding any dairy products, such as butter or parmesan. The beating in of the dairy ingredients is called the *mantecatura*.

Pancetta, Sage & Butternut Risotto

Serves 4–6

2 litres well-flavoured chicken or
  vegetable stock
2 tablespoons olive oil
10 sage leaves
5 slices pancetta or bacon, chopped into
  small pieces
3 shallots, finely chopped
1½ cups risotto rice
½ cup dry white wine
2 cups diced butternut pumpkin
  (½ cm dice)
½ cup grated parmesan, plus extra to serve
salt and freshly ground black pepper

Heat the stock to simmering in a large saucepan.

In a large deep sauté pan or saucepan, heat the olive oil and fry the sage leaves for 1 minute, until they are just dark green. Remove the leaves and drain on a paper towel.

Add the pancetta to the pan and stir until nicely browned. Remove and drain on paper towels.

Add the shallots to the pan and soften for a minute, then add the rice. Stir to coat each grain in the oily mixture.

Turn up the heat and add the wine. Stir until all the liquid evaporates. Add the hot stock, a ladle at a time, continuing to stir as the rice absorbs the stock. When half the stock has been used, add the diced butternut and stir as you continue to add the rest of the stock. After about 25 minutes, taste and check if the rice is cooked to your liking. I prefer slightly firm rice but it is a personal choice. If you use all of the stock before the rice is cooked to your liking, you can add a little more stock or hot water.

Crumple or chop half the sage leaves and add to the risotto with the crisp pancetta. Stir in the parmesan and season to taste with salt and pepper. It will need quite generous seasoning so don't be mean! Garnish with the remaining sage leaves and serve with a block of parmesan to grate or shave over.

*This risotto is a fantastic way to use the early baby vegetables of spring
— little fava (broad) beans, baby leeks and peas and so on.*

Risotto Primavera (Spring Risotto)

Serves 4–6

2 litres well-flavoured chicken or
    vegetable stock
1 cup podded baby fava (broad) beans —
    no need to peel if young, small beans
1 cup baby peas (can be frozen)
handful thin asparagus spears, trimmed
    and sliced
½ cup olive oil
100 g butter
handful thin baby leeks, finely sliced
3 spring onions, finely sliced
400 g risotto rice
½ cup dry white wine
1 tablespoon chopped Italian parsley
1 tablespoon chopped mint
½ cup grated parmesan, plus extra to serve
salt and freshly ground black pepper

Carrots
Celery

Pour the stock into a large saucepan and bring to the boil. Add the beans, peas and asparagus and cook for 2–3 minutes until tender. Drain in a colander, reserving the stock. Hold the vegetables under cold running water to cool and refresh. Return the stock to the heat and bring to a simmer.

In a large, deep sauté pan or saucepan, heat the olive oil and butter. Add the sliced leek and spring onion to the pan and cook for 2 minutes, then add the rice. Stir to coat each grain in the oily mixture.

Turn the heat up and add the wine. Stir until all the liquid evaporates. Add the hot stock, a ladle at a time, continuing to stir as the rice absorbs the stock. After about 25 minutes, taste and check if the rice is cooked to your liking. You may need to add a little extra stock or hot water.

Add the cooked vegetables, parsley and mint. Remove from heat and cool for a minute before stirring through the grated parmesan. Season with salt and pepper.

Serve in warmed bowls with a block of parmesan to grate or shave over.

Scallop & Fennel Risotto

Serves 4

2 bulbs baby fennel, trimmed
1½ litres fish stock
¼ cup olive oil
50 g butter
4 shallots, finely chopped
2 cloves garlic, crushed
1½ cups risotto rice
½ cup dry white wine
salt and freshly ground black pepper
grated rind and juice of 1 lemon
100 g butter
16 scallops, cleaned, with roe still on

Slice 1 bulb of fennel very finely on a mandolin. Chop the other bulb into fine dice like an onion.

Heat the stock to simmering in a large saucepan.

In a large, deep sauté pan or saucepan, heat the olive oil and 50 g of butter. Add the shallots, diced fennel and garlic to the pan and cook for 2 minutes to soften, then add the rice. Stir to coat each grain in the oily mixture.

Turn up the heat and add the wine. Stir until all the liquid evaporates. Add the hot stock, a ladle at a time, continuing to stir as the rice absorbs the stock. After about 25 minutes, taste and check if the rice is cooked to your liking. You may need to add a little extra stock or hot water. Season with salt and pepper, and stir in the lemon rind and juice.

Heat 100 g of butter in a small frypan. Add the finely sliced fennel and scallops to the pan and stir-fry for a minute or so until the scallops are opaque. Do not overcook. Spoon the fennel and scallop mixture over the risotto and serve in warm bowls.

Barley & Mushroom Risotto with Gremolata

Serves 4–6

For the gremolata
½ cup chopped Italian parsley
2 tablespoons finely grated lemon rind
2 cloves garlic, finely chopped

For the risotto
50 g dried porcini mushrooms
1 cup boiling water
1½ litres vegetable or chicken stock
2 tablespoons olive oil
500 g fresh mushrooms, sliced
salt and freshly ground black pepper
50 g butter
1 onion, finely chopped
1 teaspoon salt
2 cups pearl barley

Mix the gremolata ingredients together in a bowl and cover with plastic wrap.

Soak the porcini in the boiling water for 30 minutes, then strain, reserving the liquid. Chop the porcini finely.

Heat the stock to simmering in a large saucepan.

Heat the olive oil in a large sauté pan. Add the fresh mushrooms and stir until most of their liquid has evaporated and they are beginning to brown — about 5 minutes. Add the porcini mushrooms and the reserved liquid. Season generously with salt and pepper.

Tip the mushrooms and liquid into a dish and return the pan to medium-high heat. Add the butter and onion to the pan and cook for about 1 minute, then add the salt and barley. Stir to coat the barley grains in butter.

Add 1 cup of stock and stir until the liquid has evaporated. Add more stock and stir as the liquid evaporates and the barley swells. Continue until the stock is all absorbed and the barley softened. (This will take 35–40 minutes — barley takes longer to cook than rice.)

Add the mushrooms and, if necessary, extra stock or hot water until the barley grains are tender to the bite. Just before serving, mix in the gremolata. Check the seasoning. Serve hot.

Polenta can be cooked from scratch, taking about an hour and a half of very gentle simmering, but even Mamma uses instant polenta, which is ready in minutes. The important thing is a generously flavoured stock or at least lots of seasoning in the liquid, and the addition of grated parmesan and butter for a delicious creamy taste and texture.

Use polenta as you would mashed potato. It is great served as a base with casserole ladled over the top. Any leftovers can be poured into a non-stick flat dish such as a roulade or jelly-roll pan and left to set. Cut into wedges or squares and pan-fry until golden brown before serving.

Creamy Polenta

Serves 4

800 ml milk
200 ml cream
1 teaspoon flaky sea salt
1 teaspoon ground white pepper
1 cup instant polenta
1 cup grated parmesan
50 g butter

Heat the milk and cream together until just about to boil. Add the salt and pepper, and pour in the polenta in a steady stream, while you stir continuously. Continue stirring as the polenta thickens. Reduce the heat and keep stirring for 3–4 minutes. Check the seasoning.

Add the parmesan and butter and continue stirring until they have melted and the mixture is thick and the consistency of porridge.

When visiting Italy, no matter what their budget — whether they have matching luggage or a backpack — what everyone really wants is someone's Mamma or Nonna to take them home and feed them.

Pasta

Chi la sera i pasti li ha fatti,
sta agli altri lavare i piatti.

English Translation:
If one cooks the meal then
the others wash up.

Pasta Basics

The Chinese claim they were the first to discover noodle-making, and that pasta was brought to Europe by explorer Marco Polo.

However, Mamma, like most Italians, disputes this theory because the Romans and ancient Greeks ate pasta, and the climate of Italy is certainly suited to growing durum wheat. Whatever its origins, pasta is definitely an Italian staple and has been a favourite since its big rise in popularity in the fourteenth century.

All over the world there are different grades of flour but most Italians use 00 (*doppio zero*) flour for pasta. Mamma uses 00 flour and this is what I was taught to use.

00 or *doppio zero* flour has very fine particles and a high level of protein. It is milled from hard durum wheat. When you knead dough, you stretch the gluten in the flour. This makes the dough quite elastic and strengthens the pasta. Overworking can break the strands of gluten, so it is important to rest and relax the dough as soon as it forms together in a clump. Even though it feels very hard it will soften and become far more pliable once it has rested for an hour.

I have moved on to mixing 00 flour 50:50 with a fine semolina flour, which produces a wonderful pasta that has slightly more 'bite' factor — so this has become my norm.

The rule of thumb is a ratio of 100 g flour to 1 egg. It is preferable to use a nice, fresh, free-range egg which will have a rich, golden-orange yolk that will colour the pasta accordingly. Egg sizes differ slightly. I use a size 7 but a little flexibility in the rules is allowed.

The correct pasta texture comes from not only using the right type of flour but from the protein and lecithin in the eggs. They make the dough elastic, allowing the pasta to be twisted, rolled flat and shaped into many different varieties.

To Make Pasta

Serves 4

100 g 00 flour
100 g semolina flour
2 eggs

Traditionally pasta is made on a wooden surface: table, bench or board.
It helps to add texture to the finished pasta.

Sift the flours together into a pile on the bench and make a well in the middle. This is called the *fontana de farina* — the fountain of flour. Make sure the sides of the well are high enough to contain the eggs. Break the eggs into the well, then using a fork, gradually mix by flicking the flour into the egg until it forms a thick paste.

Use your fingertips to incorporate the rest of the flour. Knead well to form a firm dough. Mamma never actually adds water to the egg but sometimes she wets her hands, especially on a really warm day, as this adds a tiny bit of moisture to the dough and helps it come together.

As soon as the mixture has formed into a dough, wrap it in plastic film and allow it to relax for an hour. Even if the dough feels really hard and dry it is amazing how malleable it becomes after resting. This step is very important. Even if you are using a machine, you must rest the dough.

After resting, knead the dough to increase its elasticity. If it sticks to your hands, add just a tiny bit more flour — sufficient to stop it sticking.

Knead and work the dough for 4–5 minutes.

How to cut fresh pasta with a pasta machine

Roll out the dough with a rolling pin on a well-floured surface, or flatten it with your hands so that it will fit through the rollers of the pasta machine. Any dough you are not working with should be set aside wrapped in plastic film to prevent it drying out.

Set the machine's rollers to their widest setting and roll the dough through. Reduce the roller gap and roll through again, repeating the process until the machine is on its finest setting. Cut the pasta into manageable lengths as it gets thinner and longer.

Keep the pasta dusted with flour at all times.

If you would like to cut the pasta into tagliatelle or fettuccine, use the appropriate cutting attachments for your machine. For lasagne, cut the sheets into approximately 12 x 15 cm rectangles. The pasta can also be cut using a pastry wheel.

How to cut fresh pasta by hand

Lightly flour a wooden work surface and rolling pin. Mamma uses a long, thin wooden rolling pin but I've managed successfully with my regular one.

Roll out the pasta as thinly as possible into a large sheet. Cut in half and roll around and around the rolling pin in a tight cylinder, one half at a time. Mamma then uses her small paring knife and slits the pasta along the length of the rolling pin, then cuts these sections into tagliatelle or wider pappardelle as she requires. Then, with a gentle finger action, she breaks open the ribbons and piles them in little heaps to dry out. Sometimes she dries the lengths over a cane or broomstick or on fresh linen tea towels. Mamma says it should be dried for a short time — at least 10–15 minutes — before cooking. This may just be her little tip, however, because I've read many recipes where this step is left out and after the pasta is made it is then immediately plunged into boiling water to cook.

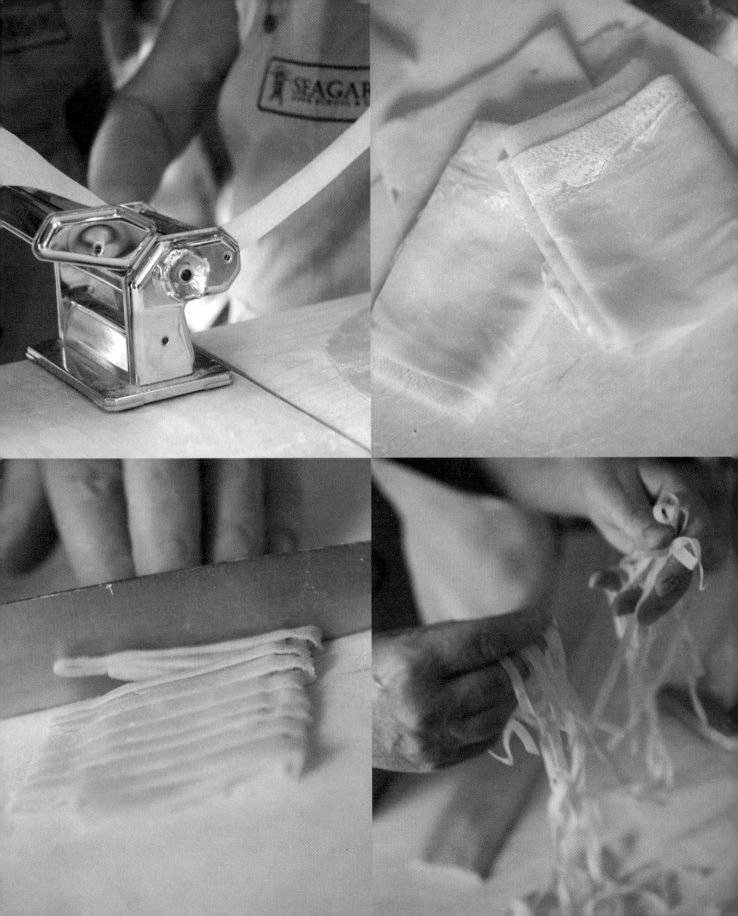

Cooking pasta

Have a large saucepan of boiling water ready. Add lots of salt — even a couple of tablespoons. The water should taste like the sea and be very buoyant. The salt helps the boiling water tumble the pasta as it cooks. Even if you are cooking only a small amount of pasta, use a big saucepan of water.

Fresh pasta will require only a minute or two of cooking to be the perfect texture — *al dente* — which means tender to the bite. The best way to check is simply to bite a piece.

Never ever put olive oil in the saucepan with the boiling water. This is a grave waste of valuable oil, and all it does is cause an oil slick on the surface of the water, preventing the lovely rolling tumble motion of the water as it evenly cooks the pasta. Also, the pasta becomes quite slimy, preventing the sauce from coating it.

Occasionally, if pasta needs to be cooked and drained and set aside for a moment, a little oil can be drizzled through it to prevent it sticking together — but never put oil in the cooking water.

Mamma nearly always makes her own pasta. Once you've made it a few times it becomes second nature. Time can be a valuable commodity, however, and good store-bought fresh or dried pasta definitely has its place. The same cooking rules apply but it will take longer to come to the al dente stage. Follow the packet's instructions and remember: lots of salt in the water, and keep tasting and testing the pasta until it is perfectly cooked.

Mamma's Quick Tomato Sauce for Pasta

Makes 6 serves

2 tablespoons olive oil

1 onion, finely chopped

3 cloves garlic, crushed

2 x 400 g cans crushed tomatoes in juice

1 tablespoon tomato paste

6 basil leaves, sliced

1 teaspoon sugar

salt and freshly ground black pepper

Heat a large frypan. Add the olive oil and onion and fry until softened. Add the garlic and cook for 1 minute, then add the tomatoes and juice, tomato paste, basil and sugar. Season with salt and pepper. Bring to the boil, then reduce the heat and simmer for 15–20 minutes.

Transfer to a blender and whiz to a sauce consistency, or use a stick blender — even Mamma uses one of these.

This is a good sauce to make in a double batch, freezing half for later.

Bolognese Sauce for Pasta

Makes 4–6 serves

25 g butter
2 tablespoons olive oil
1 onion, finely chopped
1 carrot, peeled and finely diced
1 stalk celery, finely sliced
2 cloves garlic, crushed
500 g pork mince
1 cup chopped pancetta or bacon
½ cup dry white wine
2 x 400 g cans crushed tomatoes in juice
1 cup chicken or beef stock
½ cup milk
salt and freshly ground black pepper
500 g dried or fresh pasta of your choice

Heat the butter and oil in a large saucepan over medium heat. When the butter foams, add the onion, carrot, celery and garlic. Cook until the vegetables have softened — about 6–7 minutes.

Raise the heat to high and add the pork mince and pancetta. Stir-fry until all the meat is sealed. Add the wine and stir until most of the liquid has evaporated. Add the tomatoes and juice and the stock. Bring to the boil, then reduce the heat until the mixture is just simmering. Simmer for at least an hour, then add the milk and cook for a further 30 minutes. Season with salt and pepper.

Cook the pasta and drain. Serve in a bowl, and ladle over the sauce.

Simple Zucchini Sauce for Pasta

Makes 4 serves

2 tablespoons olive oil
2 cloves garlic, crushed
2 cups grated zucchini
salt and freshly ground black pepper

Heat the olive oil in a large frypan. Add the garlic and cook for 2 minutes. Add the zucchini. Toss well in the garlic and oil to wilt. Season with salt and generous amounts of pepper, then stir through hot pasta.

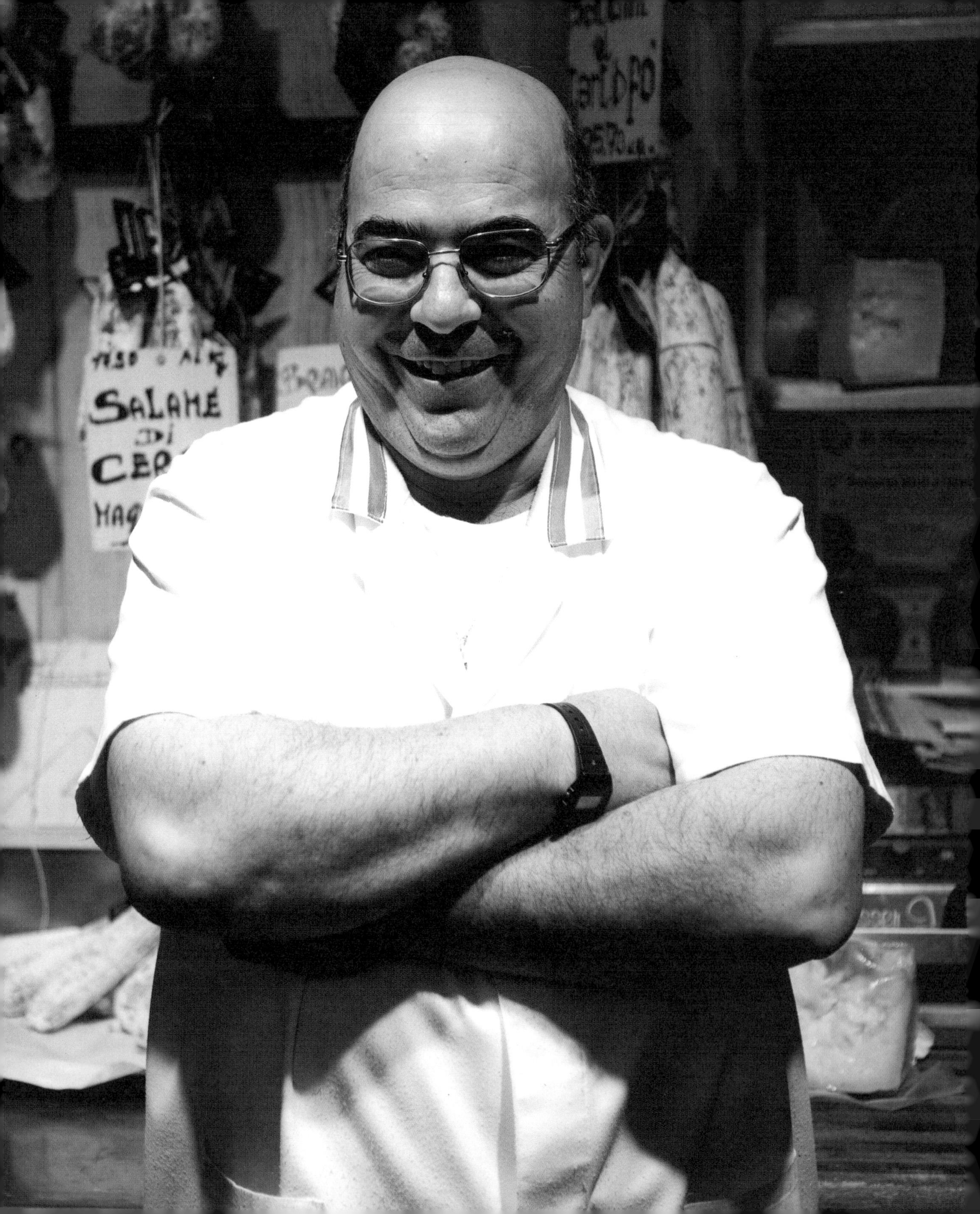
SALAME
DI

This popular recipe originated, it is believed, in the Lazio region, which has Rome as its centre. It is now available in cafés all over Italy — and indeed the world.

Spaghetti Carbonara

Serves 6

5 eggs
2 tablespoons freshly grated parmesan, plus extra to serve
2 tablespoons freshly grated pecorino
500 g dried spaghetti
1 tablespoon olive oil
25 g butter
1 cup diced pancetta or bacon (about 200 g)
2 cloves garlic, crushed
flaky sea salt and freshly ground black pepper

Whisk together the eggs, parmesan and pecorino, then set aside.

Cook the spaghetti, following the packet instructions, in a large saucepan in plenty of well-salted boiling water, until al dente.

Heat the olive oil and butter in a large frypan. Cook the diced pancetta or bacon until crisp, then add the garlic.

Drain the cooked spaghetti and return to the hot saucepan. Add the egg and cheese mixture and pancetta and garlic to the spaghetti and toss to coat. Do not return the saucepan to the heat — the egg will cook from the heat of the spaghetti alone. If you return the pan to the heat it cooks like scrambled eggs.

Season with salt and a generous grind of pepper. Serve immediately with a block of parmesan to shave over.

This is very rich but so delicious as a smaller course. Do not try to reheat this pasta or the egg-cream mixture will cook like scrambled eggs!

Penne with Garlic Cream & Breadcrumbs

Serves 4–6

300 g dried penne
50 g butter
2 cups fresh breadcrumbs, made from
   day-old bread
2 tablespoons olive oil
1 onion, finely chopped
3 cloves garlic, crushed
5 egg yolks
250 ml cream
1½ cups grated parmesan, plus extra
   to serve
salt and freshly ground black pepper
handful Italian parsley leaves, chopped

Cook the penne in a large saucepan of well-salted boiling water until al dente.

While the pasta is cooking, melt the butter over medium-high heat in a large frypan and toss the fresh breadcrumbs in it. Fry until golden brown. Turn out onto a paper towel to drain.

Wipe out the pan and place back on heat. Add the olive oil, then the onion and fry for 2–3 minutes until soft. Add the garlic and cook for a further minute.

In a small bowl, beat the egg yolks and cream together, then mix in the grated parmesan and season with salt and pepper.

Drain the pasta and return to the warm saucepan. Do not return the pan to the heat.

Pour over the contents of the frypan and the egg and cream mixture. Toss to combine. Check the seasoning — it does need a generous grind of pepper.

Just before serving in warmed bowls, stir through the parsley. Scatter the fried breadcrumbs over each serving and pass around a block of parmesan to shave over the pasta.

Pappardelle with Rocket, Fava Beans & Pancetta

Serves 4–6

For the pappardelle
400 g 00 flour
4 eggs

For the sauce
500 g fresh or frozen fava (broad) beans
2 tablespoons olive oil
100 g pancetta or streaky bacon, finely sliced
1 onion, finely chopped
1 clove garlic, crushed
½ cup white wine
3 tablespoons cream
salt and freshly ground black pepper
2 handfuls wild rocket leaves
parmesan to serve

Make a double batch of basic pasta (see instructions on page 156), then cut into long, flat strips 2–2.5 cm wide. Lay batches of the cut strips on a well-floured tray to prevent them sticking while you roll the rest of the dough through the pasta machine.

If the fava beans are fresh, bring a saucepan of salted water to the boil and cook for 4–5 minutes until softened. Drain and plunge into cold water, then peel off the grey outer skins. (If the broad beans are frozen, defrost and peel. They won't need any further cooking.)

Heat the olive oil in a large frypan. Add the sliced pancetta or bacon and onion. Stir-fry until the onion has softened and the pancetta cooked — about 5 minutes. Add the garlic and cook for another minute, then add the white wine. Stir well while it reduces and evaporates.

Bring a large saucepan of well-salted water to the boil and cook the pasta. It should only need 2–3 minutes to become al dente. Drain and return to the hot saucepan.

Just before serving, add the cream to the onions and pancetta. Season with a little salt and lots of pepper. Tip into the saucepan of pasta and toss together. Serve in warmed bowls. Sprinkle over the rocket leaves and pass around a block of parmesan to shave over the pasta.

Tagliatelle with Lemon, Garlic & Parmesan

Serves 4

400 g fresh tagliatelle
¼ cup extra virgin olive oil
3 cloves garlic, crushed
grated rind and juice of 2 lemons
1 cup freshly grated parmesan
½ cup cream
handful Italian parsley, chopped
salt and freshly ground black pepper

Bring a large saucepan of water to the boil. Add generous amounts of salt and, when boiling again, add the tagliatelle. Cook until al dente — just a few minutes should do it. Drain in a colander.

Place the extra virgin olive oil and garlic into the hot pasta saucepan. Cook for about 1 minute, then add the lemon rind and juice, parmesan, cream and parsley, and season with salt and pepper. Return the drained pasta to the saucepan. Mix well and serve immediately in warmed bowls.

Baked Tagliatelle with Asparagus, Lemon, Pinenuts & Mascarpone

Serves 4

1 kg medium-sized asparagus spears,
  sliced into 2–3 cm pieces on an angle
2 tablespoons olive oil
10 spring onions, sliced
grated rind and juice of 2 lemons
fresh thyme leaves
salt and freshly ground black pepper
25 g butter
1 tablespoon flour
1 cup milk
1 cup mascarpone
1 cup grated Grana Padano
1 cup coarse fresh breadcrumbs
500 g fresh tagliatelle
½ cup pinenuts

Preheat the oven to 200°C. Spray a 20 x 30 cm lasagne dish or four individual ovenproof bowls with non-stick baking spray or olive oil.

Bring a large saucepan of salted water to the boil. Blanch the asparagus for 2 minutes, then remove with a slotted spoon to a colander or sieve and run under cold water to preserve the bright green colour. Keep the water boiling for the pasta.

In a large frypan, heat the olive oil and sauté the spring onions for 1 minute. Add the drained asparagus and sauté for a further minute. Add the lemon juice and half the rind, thyme leaves and salt and pepper. Remove from the heat.

In a medium saucepan, heat the butter and whisk in the flour. Cook for 20–30 seconds, stirring with the whisk. Slowly, while whisking continuously, add the milk and stir until it comes to the boil. Lower the heat and whisk in the remaining lemon rind, the mascarpone and half the Grana Padano. Whisk until really smooth and the cheese is melted and combined. Season with salt and pepper.

Continued

In a small bowl, mix the breadcrumbs with the remaining Grana Padano, salt and pepper and a little drizzle of olive oil. Mix really well.

With the pasta water really boiling, add the tagliatelle and cook for a few minutes until slightly underdone. Drain well.

Mix together the pasta, cheese sauce, asparagus mixture and pinenuts. Pour into the prepared dish or dishes and sprinkle over the breadcrumb mixture. Bake for 15–20 minutes until bubbling and golden brown. Serve immediately.

Tartufo (Truffles)

Truffles are fungi, distant cousins of the mushroom. They are hypogenic — which means they live completely underground. They grow only in certain soils near the roots of trees. The type of tree and soil determines the flavour and quintessential aroma of the truffles. Experts can tell you what kind of tree they grew alongside just from their smell and taste.

There are two main groups of truffles — black and white — but lots of species of each.

Italy harvests about seventeen varieties. Its main competitor is France, which produces the famous black Périgord truffle.

The Tuber magnatum pico is a rare and very valuable white truffle. Its aroma and flavour are very pungent and it is known as the king of truffles. These are never cooked but only served fresh, shaved over warm dishes.

The black truffle or *tartufo nero* is more common and usually weighs between 20 and 100 g. They are harvested for a longer season than the white truffle, and they keep better and for longer. Wrap them in cloth such as muslin and store them in the fridge in a screw-top jar, to stop them flavouring other foods, especially eggs. Black truffles are less expensive than white and can be chopped or sliced into dishes and sauces and also used to flavour oil.

Truffle hunters — *trifulau* — look for the fungi with the aid of specially trained dogs. Pigs were used in the past but while they found the truffles all right, they then ate them! Dogs can be trained to just locate truffles and bark to indicate their whereabouts. Black and white truffles, and truffle oil, are available in New Zealand from specialist Italian food importers, good delis and gourmet food stores.

Tagliatelle with Truffle Sauce

Serves 4

¼ cup olive oil

4 cloves garlic, peeled and cut into
   2–3 pieces each

400 g fresh tagliatelle

2 black truffles the size of golf balls, finely
   grated or finely sliced using a truffle
   mandolin

salt and freshly ground black pepper

Heat the oil in a large frypan over medium-high heat and add the chopped garlic. Remove from the heat and allow the oil to cool, then scoop or strain out the garlic and discard. (Mamma adds the garlic to her stockpot — nothing is wasted.) Set aside.

Bring a large saucepan of water to the boil. Add generous amounts of salt and, when boiling again, add the tagliatelle. Cook until al dente — just a few minutes should do it. Drain in a colander.

Heat the garlic oil in a large pan and add the truffle. When sizzling hot, toss with the drained pasta. Season with salt and pepper to taste and mix well to coat each strand of pasta in truffle oil.

Farfalle is butterly or bow-tie-shaped pasta.

Farfalle with Tomato, Basil & Broccoli Butter

Serves 4–6

500 g dried farfalle pasta
1 head broccoli
2 cups chicken stock
100 g butter
2 cups cherry tomatoes, halved
handful basil leaves
flaky sea salt and freshly ground black
  pepper

Cook the pasta following the packet instructions until al dente. Meanwhile, trim the broccoli into small, bite-sized florets, peeling the stalks and using the stem as well as the flower part.

Heat the stock in a small saucepan to a simmer and add the broccoli. As soon as the broccoli is tender, remove it with a slotted spoon. Save the stock for a soup.

When the pasta is cooked, drain in a colander. Melt the butter in the hot pasta saucepan. Add the tender broccoli, cherry tomatoes and, using scissors, snip the basil leaves into shreds over the pan. Return the drained pasta to the saucepan and toss well. Season with salt and pepper.

Ravioli

These are the most famous of the filled or stuffed pastas.

Traditionally, ravioli made in the northern part of Italy were filled with meat while cooks in the south filled theirs with vegetables. Ravioli from coastal regions had a seafood filling. Nowadays anything and everything can be used as the filling.

I am not sure what Mamma would think of my paua-filled ravioli or the ravioli containing scallops and Japanese pickled ginger slices that I have been experimenting with but, really, anything goes.

Hand-made pasta parcels with fluted edges, made with a pastry roller, are known as ravioli. Those with plain edges, just cut with a knife, are known as tordelli or tortelli.

Filled pastas are perfect to freeze — just separate and free-flow freeze them. Store in a plastic container in the freezer, then cook from frozen.

Spinach & Ricotta Ravioli

Serves 4–6

For the ravioli
100 g 00 flour
100 g semolina flour
2 eggs

For the filling
150 g spinach
300 g firm ricotta, drained through a sieve
  or piece of muslin if very wet
1 cup finely grated parmesan
½ teaspoon freshly grated nutmeg
flaky sea salt and freshly ground black
  pepper

Prepare basic pasta dough as per instructions on page 156.

Plunge the spinach into boiling water (or microwave) to wilt. Drain and squeeze out the excess water. Place in a food processor with the ricotta, parmesan, nutmeg and salt and pepper. Process to mix thoroughly. Taste to check the seasoning.

Roll out a section of the pasta, keeping the remaining dough in the plastic wrap so that it does not dry out. Roll through the pasta machine to the thinnest or second thinnest setting. Cut the lengths in half for ease of handling and keep the work surface well floured. Dust only the underside of the dough with flour, not the top, as you want it to stick to the other half of the ravioli.

Use semolina flour for dusting benches and flouring work surfaces. It has an ever-so-slightly gritty texture which makes it easier to roll the dough out and helps to prevent sticking.

For larger ravioli

Spread a length of rolled pasta on the floured surface. Place heaped teaspoons of filling along the length, about 2 cm apart, allowing room to cut out shapes but not to waste too much pasta.

Lay a second sheet of pasta, non-floured surface face down, on top of the first sheet. Press gently down around each individual mound to expel any air and seal. Cut around each the raviolo (singular) with a pastry wheel or use a special ravioli cutter — like a cookie cutter. Some are square and some round.

Place the finished ravioli on a well-floured tray while you make the rest.

For smaller ravioli

Lots of people, including Mamma, have a special ravioli press that makes about 20 bite-sized pieces at once. The very important thing with this method is to thoroughly flour the press first, before laying the first sheet of pasta onto it.

Press the pasta into the indentations with your fingers. Place tiny spoonfuls of filling — about a ½ teaspoonful — into each mould. Place the second sheet of pasta, floured side up, on top. Run a rolling pin firmly over the surface to force the filling down into the moulds. Turn the press over and bang it down firmly on the bench to release the sheet of ravioli, then cut with a ravioli cutter or knife into individual portions. Keep these on a well-floured tray while you complete the batch.

To cook ravioli

This is very similar to cooking other types of pasta.

Bring a large saucepan of water to the boil. Add lots of salt — even a couple of tablespoons. The water should taste like the sea and be very buoyant. The salt helps the boiling water tumble the pasta as it cooks.

Add the ravioli and cook for 3–4 minutes until al dente. Drain in a colander and add to the sauce.

Mamma says to always heat pasta plates. This is very important and my real 'mamma' agrees — it is obviously a 'mother' thing.

Ravioli with Sage Butter Sauce

Serves 6

200 g butter
12 fresh sage leaves
1 portion Spinach & Ricotta Ravioli
  (see page 196)
salt and freshly ground black pepper

Cook the ravioli in boiling salted water until al dente. Drain in a colander.

Heat the butter in a small frypan. When melted, add the fresh sage leaves and sizzle in the butter, being careful not to let them burn.

Return the hot pasta to the saucepan, pour over the sizzling sage butter and season with salt and pepper. Serve on warm plates.

Herb & Ricotta Ravioli with Walnut Sauce

Serves 4

For the ravioli
100 g 00 flour
100 g semolina flour
2 eggs

For the filling
1 tablespoon olive oil
2 large bunches Italian parsley
10–12 fresh basil leaves
4 sage leaves
small handful fresh oregano leaves
2 handfuls baby spinach leaves
400 g fresh ricotta
1 cup grated parmesan
1 egg

For the walnut sauce
50 g butter
½ cup walnut halves
2 tablespoons walnut oil
1 clove garlic, crushed
salt and freshly ground black pepper
Italian parsley leaves, chopped, to garnish

Prepare the basic pasta dough as per the instructions on page 156.

Heat a large frypan over medium-high heat. Add the olive oil, all the herbs and the spinach. Soften and wilt the greens for 2 minutes, then drain in a sieve, pressing down with a spoon to remove all excess liquid.

Place the drained herbs and spinach in a food proces-sor with the ricotta, parmesan and egg. Whiz to a smooth paste.

Fill and cook the ravioli as per the instructions on page 196.

To make the walnut sauce, heat a small frypan and add all the ingredients except the parsley. Sizzle for 3–4 minutes to toast and slightly brown the walnuts. Pour over the cooked ravioli and garnish with chopped parsley leaves.

Tortellini

These are small filled pasta that are folded and twisted to resemble tummy buttons —
supposedly the inspiration for these was the tummy button of Venus. Larger versions are
called tortelloni.

Make the basic pasta dough and follow the instructions for making ravioli (see page 196)
until you've rolled out the long sheets of pasta. Now cut them into 6 cm squares. Dot a
teaspoon of filling onto each square and fold it to form a triangle. Press the pasta firmly
around the filling, expelling the air. Fold two of the triangle points around your finger,
pressing to make the traditional shape. Flick the third little triangle corner over like a hat.

Cook tortellini as you would ravioli.

Tortellini with Brown Butter Sage Sauce & Parmesan

Serves 4

1 portion Spinach & Ricotta Tortellini
(see page 196 for filling and 205 for
tortellini instructions)
2 tablespoons olive oil
200 g butter
12–18 fresh sage leaves
salt and freshly ground black pepper
parmesan to serve

Cook the tortellini in boiling salted water until al dente.

Heat the olive oil in a large frypan. Add the butter and melt it to sizzling. (The oil helps to prevent the butter burning.) Add the sage leaves and fry for 2–3 minutes. Season with salt and generous amounts of pepper.

Drain the tortellini and return to the hot saucepan. Drizzle the sage butter over and toss to mix well.

Serve on warm plates, making sure each portion has a sage leaf or 2. Shave over parmesan to serve.

Agnolotti are another pasta shape made in exactly the same way as ravioli. Usually they are round, but as with everything foody in Italy, there are thousands of variations, and every Italian swears theirs is the true original. Mamma makes hers round — I make mine round. The spinach and ricotta filling is particularly good with radicchio sauce.

Agnolotti with Radicchio Sauce

Serves 4

1 portion Spinach & Ricotta Agnolotti
  (see ravioli recipe page 196)
1 small onion, finely chopped
2–3 medium radicchio, finely sliced
3 tablespoons olive oil
½ cup chicken or vegetable stock
salt and freshly ground black pepper
shaved parmesan to serve

Cook the agnolotti in boiling salted water until al dente.

Heat the olive oil in a large frypan and fry the onion for 3–4 minutes until softened. Add the sliced radicchio, stirring until it has wilted.

Add the stock and allow it to sizzle and reduce for a few minutes. Season to taste with salt and pepper.

Add the hot, cooked and drained agnolotti and mix through. Serve with shavings of parmesan and an extra grind of pepper.

Italian families tend to live close together so eating together happens often. They follow the traditions and recipes learned from the previous generations.

Bread

I have adapted this recipe to use dried yeast granules, as it is difficult to get fresh yeast like Mamma uses — you could try a bakery if you want to give it a go.

Mamma's Pizza Base

Makes 2–3 pizza bases

1 tablespoon dried yeast granules
¾ cup warm water — about 36°C or
   baby-bath temperature
pinch caster sugar
2¾ cups high-grade flour, plus extra
   for dusting
1 teaspoon salt
1 tablespoon extra virgin olive oil

Mix the yeast, water and caster sugar in a small bowl and leave for 10 minutes until frothy.

Place the flour and salt on the bench in a small pile. Make a well in the centre and pour the yeast mixture and the oil into the well. Using a fork, flick the flour around the edges into the liquid in the centre and gradually mix it all together to form the dough.

Lightly dust the board or bench and knead the dough until quite silky and elastic. This will take about 10 minutes of decent hard work — pushing away with the heel of your hand and gathering it up again. No mucking about or resting!

Brush the inside of a large bowl with olive oil and place the dough in it. Cover with plastic wrap and place somewhere warm — we put ours out on the sun-warmed steps — until doubled in size, about 1½–2 hours.

Punch the dough down and work it again, kneading and shaping or rolling into flattened circles about 5 mm thick. Transfer the discs to an oven tray or pizza stone. Cover with a tea towel for a further 20 minutes while you preheat the oven to 200°C. Top with whatever you like and bake for 10–15 minutes, depending on the toppings.

Italian pizza toppings are very simple — always just one or two flavours. Most pizzas have a tomato sauce base, then a second topping. For example, mozzarella, finely chopped sausage, thinly sliced courgette or mushroom. Always add a drizzle of olive oil and lots of salt.

Fresh Tomato Sauce for Pizza

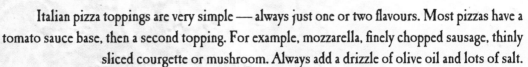

Roma tomatoes
salt and freshly ground black pepper
fresh oregano (or dried if fresh
   not available)

Preheat the oven to 150°C.

Roughly chop up the tomatoes and salt heavily. Spread in a shallow roasting tray. Sprinkle with pepper and oregano.

Place in the oven for about half an hour, then mash a little with a fork, then place back in the oven for another half to three-quarters of an hour. The oven helps to evaporate the liquid, giving a thick, concentrated sauce. If desired you can purée the tomatoes in a blender.

Mamma's big tip — less topping is best, but don't be mean with the salt.

Tomato Mozzarella & Rocket Pizza

1 portion pizza dough (see page 216)
fresh tomato sauce (see page 219)

Preheat the oven to 220°C or prepare a pizza oven if you have one.

Place the prepared pizza base on a pizza stone or large oven tray. Spread with a layer of tomato sauce, leaving the outer 1½ cm edge free of sauce. Top with a few slices of mozzarella. Cook for approximately 10 minutes, until the edges are puffy and browned. The hotter the oven the faster and better it will cook.

Sprinkle a few rocket leaves over the hot pizza. Serve cut into wedges.

This is one of the easiest breads to make. Mamma of course does it all by hand, but I make mine using the cake mixer fitted with a dough hook, or even in a large food processor — anything for speedy preparation.

Focaccia

1 tablespoon dried yeast granules

½ teaspoon caster sugar

1¾ cups warm water — about 36 °C or baby-bath temperature

4½ cups 00 or high-grade flour

½ cup extra virgin olive oil

1 tablespoon flaky sea salt, plus extra to sprinkle

In either a large bowl, electric mixer or food processor bowl, place the dried yeast, caster sugar and warm water. Leave for 10 minutes for the yeast to start working. You will see bubbles and froth starting to form on the surface.

Add the flour, half the olive oil, and salt and mix, beat or process to a soft dough. Flour your hands and knead for a few minutes until the dough is silky smooth.

Take a large bowl, big enough for the dough to double in size, and brush or spray with olive oil. Roll the dough in the bowl to coat with the oil. Cover with a tea towel or wrap in plastic and place in a warm, draught-free area for the dough to rise — about 1 hour.

Thoroughly oil a large 40 x 30 cm slice or sponge roll tray. Punch down the dough and knead again for a few minutes. Press the dough into the prepared tray. Allow the dough to rise again in a warm place for half an hour.

Preheat the oven to 200°C.

Drizzle the bread with the remainder of the olive oil and sprinkle with the sea salt. Bake for 20–25 minutes until risen and golden brown.

Cool on a wire rack.

You can also sprinkle over little sprigs of fresh thyme or rosemary, or sliced olives before cooking, in addition to the olive oil and sea salt.

Grissini (Breadsticks)

Makes 20

½ cup warm water — about 36°C
   or baby-bath temperature
1 tablespoon olive oil
2 teaspoons dried yeast granules
½ teaspoon sugar
1 teaspoon salt
1½ cups high-grade or 00 flour
sesame seeds, poppy seeds or flaky
   sea salt (optional)

Mix the water, olive oil, yeast, sugar and salt in a large bowl. Stand for 10 minutes until the mixture is bubbling and frothy.

Add the flour and mix well to form a dough. Then knead for a few minutes into a smooth, soft dough, adding extra flour if required. Place the dough in an oiled bowl and cover with plastic wrap. Leave the bowl in a warm, draught-free place and allow the dough to rise until it has doubled in size — about 1–1½ hours. A sunny windowsill or warming cupboard are good spots.

Preheat the oven to 180°C. Spray an oven tray with non-stick baking spray or brush with oil.

Punch the dough down and knead for 3–4 minutes, then shape into 20 x 20–25 cm long sausage-shaped breadsticks. Place the breadsticks in rows on the prepared tray. If desired, sprinkle with sesame or poppy seeds or sea salt. Bake for 20–25 minutes until crisp and golden brown. Cool on a wire rack.

These are a delicious surprise — little rolls with a salty anchovy filling cooked crispy-golden in the oven. Traditionally they may have been fried like a savoury doughnut.

Panini alle Acciughe (Anchovy Rolls)

Makes 15

1 cup 00 or high-grade flour
1½ teaspoons flaky sea salt
2 tablespoons olive oil
1 tablespoon dried yeast granules
150 ml warm water — about 36°C
   or baby-bath temperature
½ teaspoon caster sugar
15 anchovies
15 fresh basil leaves

Mix the flour and salt together in a bowl. Make a well in the centre and add the olive oil, yeast, warm water and sugar. Leave for 5 minutes then mix together to form a soft dough. Knead on a lightly floured bench for 5 minutes.

Place the dough in an oiled bowl and cover with plastic wrap. Leave the bowl in a warm, draught-free place and allow the dough to rise until it has doubled in size — about 1–1½ hours. A sunny windowsill or warming cupboard are good spots.

Divide the dough into 15 pieces and roll into small, even-sized balls. Flatten the balls and place an anchovy and a basil leaf in the centre of each. Pinch the dough over, enclosing the anchovy and basil.

Spray an oven tray with non-stick baking spray.

Lay the rolls on the prepared tray. Cover with a sheet of oiled plastic wrap and allow to rise for 30 minutes.

Preheat the oven to 200°C.

Remove the plastic wrap and bake the rolls for 12–15 minutes until golden brown. Cool on a wire rack.

Piadina (Flatbreads)

Makes 10

1 teaspoon salt
4 cups flour
2 teaspoons baking powder
40 g lard, cut into little pieces
olive oil for brushing

Sift the salt, flour and baking powder into a bowl. Rub in the lard. This can be done in a food processor or cake mixer. Mix in enough warm water (baby-bath temperature) to make a soft dough. Cover the bowl with a clean tea towel or plastic wrap and leave for 30 minutes.

Knead the dough and divide into 10 balls. Roll out each ball into a thin saucer shape.

Heat a large frypan and brush with a little olive oil. Fry each piadina for 2–3 minutes each side, until just lightly browned.

Serve with sliced cheese and prosciutto, folding in half to eat.

Ciabatta can also be baked on a pizza stone if you have one.

Ciabatta means 'slipper', so this bread is shaped like a flat slipper or shoe. It is a very common Italian bread and quite easy to make — although it appears to be complicated. The dough is very soft and quite sticky but don't be tempted to add more flour. It produces a lovely crispy crust and a spongy-crumbed loaf. You need to make the starter or 'sponge' 12 hours ahead of baking the bread.

Ciabatta

Makes 2 loaves

For the sponge
1 cup warm water — about 36°C
   or baby-bath temperature
1 teaspoon dried yeast granules
1½ cups high-grade or 00 flour

For the bread
1½ teaspoons dried yeast granules
5 tablespoons milk
1 cup warm water
1 tablespoon olive oil
3 cups high-grade or 00 flour
2 teaspoons salt

To make the sponge, stir together the warm water and yeast. Set aside for 10 minutes until frothy and foaming. Add the flour and mix well. Cover the bowl with plastic wrap and leave for 12 hours or overnight.

To make the bread, place all the ingredients in a large bowl. Add in the sponge mixture. Mamma mixes this together by hand but I use the dough hook on my cake mixer. Whichever method you use, knead the dough until smooth, very soft and well mixed.

Place the dough in an oiled bowl and cover with plastic wrap. Leave the bowl in a warm, draught-free place to allow the dough to rise until it has doubled in size — about 1–1½ hours. A sunny windowsill or warming cupboard are good spots. The dough will be quite sticky and full of bubbles.

Spray a large oven tray with non-stick baking spray and sprinkle with flour. Divide the dough in 2 and shape into long, oval loaves. Dust each with flour and place on the prepared trays. Cover with oiled plastic wrap and leave to rise for 1 hour, until doubled in size.

Preheat the oven to 200°C. Bake the loaves in the oven for 20–25 minutes. Spray with a fine mist of water twice during cooking. Cool on a wire rack, covered with a tea towel. This gives the bread the desired crust.

Mamma always says you have to cook with the best ingredients and be brave with the food!

Meat, Chicken, Game & Fish

A simple chicken breast topped with prosciutto and sage in a wine sauce — easy but very delicious. It's great with soft polenta or mashed potato.

Chicken Saltimbocca

Serves 4

4 boneless, skinless chicken breasts
salt and freshly ground black pepper
3 tablespoons extra virgin olive oil
50 g butter
24 large fresh sage leaves
4 slices prosciutto, cut crossways into
   thin strips
1 cup white wine
1 cup chicken stock

Trim away excess fat from the chicken and remove the tenderloins if still attached. Reserve for another use. Place the breasts between 2 sheets of plastic wrap and, using a smooth meat mallet or small heavy frypan, pound the breasts until they are about 1 cm thick. Season with salt and pepper.

Heat the oil and butter in a large non-stick frypan over medium-high heat. Fry the chicken for 3–4 minutes on each side to brown and cook through. Remove the chicken and add the sage leaves and prosciutto to the pan. Cook about 1 minute until the prosciutto is crisp and slightly browned. Transfer to paper towels and blot off the excess fat.

Drain the fat from the pan and return to the heat. Pour in the wine and bring to the boil, scraping any browned bits from the surface of the pan. Add the chicken stock and stir as it reduces to approximately 1 cup of sauce.

Serve the chicken with the sauce poured over and the crispy sage and prosciutto arranged on top.

Mamma uses lovely veal cutlets but this recipe also works well with pork or chicken.

Breaded Scaloppini

Serves 4

4 veal cutlets
½ cup flour
salt and freshly ground black pepper
2 cups fresh breadcrumbs, made from
    day-old bread
1 tablespoon finely chopped Italian
    parsley
grated rind of 1 lemon
2 eggs
¼ cup oil
50 g butter

For the salad dressing
3 tablespoons extra virgin olive oil
2 tablespoons balsamic vinegar
flaky sea salt and freshly ground black
    pepper

salad leaves to serve
lemon wedges to serve

Using a small heavy frypan or smooth meat mallet, pound the cutlets between 2 sheets of plastic wrap until they are about 1 cm thick.

Season the flour generously with salt and pepper and place in a plastic bag. Place the breadcrumbs, parsley and lemon rind in a second plastic bag. Beat the eggs in a bowl.

Place the pounded cutlets in the flour bag and shake to coat well. Dip them in the beaten egg before dropping, 1 at a time, into the breadcrumbs bag. Press the crumbs firmly into the meat to make them stick well. Chill the crumbed cutlets in the fridge for half an hour before cooking.

Heat the oil and butter in a large frypan. Once sizzling, cook the scaloppini until golden brown, then turn and cook the other side.

To make the dressing, whisk the olive oil, vinegar and salt and pepper together in a cup or small bowl. Drizzle over the salad greens just before serving. Toss to coat evenly.

Serve scaloppini on a bed of salad greens with a wedge of lemon to squeeze over.

Chicken Involtini with Mozzarella, Sage & Lemon

Serves 6

3 large boneless, skinless chicken breasts

2 x 250 g balls buffalo mozzarella, cut into 12 thin slices

2 handfuls sage leaves (approximately 24 leaves)

grated rind of 2 lemons

12 slices prosciutto

150 g butter

2 tablespoons olive oil

Preheat the oven to 200°C.

Cut each chicken breast lengthways into 4 pieces. Place the strips between 2 sheets of plastic wrap and pound flat with a meat mallet or a small heavy frypan.

Lay each chicken piece on a work surface, top with a slice of mozzarella, a fresh sage leaf and spinkle with lemon rind. Roll up, then wrap in a slice of prosciutto, enclosing a second sage leaf in the wrap. Secure with a toothpick if required.

Heat the butter and oil in a large frypan over medium-high heat. Pan-fry the involtini parcels for a few minutes on each side, until they just start to colour. Transfer to a baking dish. Add the pan juices. Roast for 10–15 minutes until the chicken is cooked through.

Fish Baked with Fennel, Lemon & Capers

Serves 6

6 fillets firm-fleshed white fish, boneless
   and skinless
3 bulbs fennel, sliced thinly (a mandolin
   is very useful for slicing)
¼ cup olive oil
3 cloves garlic, crushed
2 lemons, thinly sliced
1 tablespoon dried oregano
½ cup capers, rinsed
1 cup white wine
2 tablespoons chopped Italian parsley
lemon wedges to serve

Preheat the oven to 180°C.

Wash the fish fillets and pat dry on paper towels.

Heat a large ovenproof frypan over medium heat. Add the fennel and olive oil. Stir-fry for 5–6 minutes to soften and cook the fennel. Add the garlic and lemon slices. Cook for another 2 minutes. Place the fish on top of the fennel mixture and sprinkle with the oregano and capers. Pour over the white wine. Place in the oven and bake for 12–15 minutes.

Serve sprinkled with the chopped parsley and fresh lemon wedges to squeeze over.

Pancetta-wrapped Meatloaves with Tomato Sauce

Serves 6

¼ cup olive oil

2 large onions, finely chopped

4 cloves garlic, crushed

1 tablespoon chopped fresh oregano

2 fresh sage leaves, finely chopped

salt and freshly ground black pepper

500 g minced pork

500 g minced beef

2 eggs

1 cup fresh breadcrumbs, made from
   day-old bread

½ cup grated parmesan

12 wide, flat slices pancetta or streaky
   bacon

2 x 400 g cans crushed tomatoes in juice

1 cup red wine

Heat the olive oil in a large frypan and cook the onions and garlic until soft and translucent. Stir in the herbs and season with salt and pepper. Set aside to cool.

Preheat the oven to 180°C.

Combine the minced meats, eggs, breadcrumbs and parmesan. Then add in the cooled onion mixture. (Mamma does this by hand but I do it in a food processor.)

Divide the mixture into 12 balls and shape into little logs. Wrap each log in a rasher of pancetta. Place in a deep casserole dish.

Mix the tomatoes and wine together and season well. Pour over the meatloaves and bake for 40–45 minutes. Turn the meatloaves once or twice during cooking and check the tomato sauce is still liquid — top up with water or extra wine if required.

Costolette di Agnello al Burro di Acciughe (Lamb Cutlets with Anchovy Butter)

Serves 4

150 g butter, softened to room
   temperature
50 g anchovy fillets, rinsed
1 teaspoon anchovy paste
1 tablespoon Italian parsley, chopped
12 lamb cutlets
olive oil
salt and freshly ground black pepper

To make the anchovy butter, process the softened butter with the anchovy fillets, paste and parsley. Mix until smoothly combined.

Brush both sides of the cutlets with olive oil and generously season with salt and pepper. Barbecue or grill the cutlets for 3–4 minutes on each side.

Transfer the cutlets to a serving plate and serve with anchovy butter dotted over or on the side.

Pheasant is available from specialist game butchers.

Pheasant Braised in Red Wine with Grapes

Serves 4

2 pheasants, plucked and dressed

¼ cup olive oil

1 onion, roughly chopped

5 cloves garlic, squashed with the blade of
  a knife and roughly chopped

100 g pancetta, finely chopped

3 stalks celery, finely sliced

3 carrots, peeled and finely diced

25 g dried porcini mushrooms

10 cm branch rosemary

6 fresh bay leaves

1 bottle red wine

2 tablespoons balsamic vinegar

3 cups seedless red grapes

¼ cup chopped Italian parsley

Preheat the oven to 160°C.

Cut the pheasants into quarters and rinse. Heat the oil in a heavy casserole dish on the stovetop. Brown the pheasant quarters in batches and set aside. Add the onion, garlic and pancetta to the casserole dish and cook for 5 minutes, stirring. Add the celery and carrots.

Soak the mushrooms for 10 minutes in boiling water. Drain, reserving the water, and chop. Add the mushrooms and water to the casserole dish, along with the rosemary, bay leaves and wine.

Return the pheasant to the dish, cover with a lid and cook in the oven for 3 hours, stirring every now and again and topping up the liquid with water if required.

Remove from the oven and stir in the vinegar and grapes. Garnish with chopped parsley and serve with mashed potato or creamy polenta.

Duck Breast Salad with Fava Beans & Rocket

Serves 4

2 duck breasts, skin on
2 handfuls young rocket leaves
2 cups fava (broad) beans, cooked
  and peeled
1 cup sliced cherry tomatoes
grated rind and juice of 1 blood orange
1 tablespoon extra virgin olive oil
flaky sea salt and freshly ground black
  pepper
2 tablespoons Italian parsley

Heat a small frypan until very hot. There is no need for any oil. Score the skin side of the duck breasts in fine lines, just cutting through the fat, not the flesh. Place the breasts, skin-side down, in the pan. Sear for a timed 4 minutes.

Place the rocket leaves on 4 serving plates. Divide the fava beans and cherry tomatoes over the rocket. Whisk the orange rind and juice and olive oil together in a small bowl. Season with salt and pepper.

Turn the breasts and cook for 3 more minutes. Remove to a plate to rest for 5 minutes before slicing thinly.

Scatter the duck over the salad and drizzle with the dressing. Sprinkle with parsley.

Pork Fillets with Grapes, White Wine & Rosemary

Serves 4–6

2 pork fillets, trimmed of any sinew
and fat
2 tablespoons olive oil
1 cup chopped shallots
3 cloves garlic, crushed
2 tablespoons wholegrain mustard
10 cm branch rosemary
2 cups white wine
2 cups small seedless black grapes
250 g crème fraîche
fresh rosemary sprigs to garnish

Heat a large non-stick frypan over medium-high heat and cook the fillets for 6–7 minutes, turning to brown evenly. You may have to cut them in half if they are too large for the pan. Remove after cooking and rest in a warm place under a sheet of tinfoil.

Add the olive oil to the pan and return to the heat. Sauté the shallots and garlic for 5–6 minutes to soften and lightly caramelise. Add the mustard, rosemary branch and wine. Turn the heat down a little to bubble and reduce the sauce to about 1 cup. Remove the rosemary — don't worry if a few leaves have come off the branch.

Add the grapes and stir in the crème fraîche. Return the pork to the sauce to gently reheat. Do not boil — just warm up the meat.

Slice the meat and serve on warm plates, with the grapes and sauce spooned over the top. Garnish with a fresh sprig of rosemary.

Steak with Gorgonzola

Grill on the barbecue or pan-fry 3–4 cm thick fillet steaks — Mamma says 3 minutes each side for pink medium rare. Remove the steaks to a serving plate.

Mash a generous slice of Gorgonzola onto the top of each steak. This melts and oozes down the sides like a delicious sauce. Add a good grind of black pepper and they are complete.

Couldn't be easier or more fantastic!

Tagliata di Manzo (Sliced Steak Salad with Rosemary & Green Peppercorns)

Serves 6

4 x 15 cm branches fresh rosemary
6 cloves garlic
½ cup extra virgin olive oil
3 sirloin or Scotch fillet steaks, at least
  4 cm thick
flaky sea salt
2 tablespoons green peppercorns
  in brine, drained
salad greens to serve

Pull all of the rosemary leaves off the branches and chop finely. Crush the garlic and mix with the rosemary leaves and olive oil.

Heat the garlic, rosemary and olive oil mixture in a small saucepan over medium heat until quite hot — about 2–3 minutes. Cool completely. Strain and discard the solids.

Barbecue or pan-fry the steaks for 2–3 minutes each side, then remove from the heat and cool completely. They will be rare and quite pink inside.

Cut the cooled steaks into thin slices and lay on a serving platter. Sprinkle over the garlic rosemary oil, salt and peppercorns.

Serve with a green salad containing lots of rocket and cress or peppery herbs.

Rustic Pork Sausages with White Beans, Tomato & Bay Leaves

Serves 6

¼ cup olive oil

1 large onion, finely sliced

4 cloves garlic, crushed

500 g pork sausages (pork and fennel are good if you can get them)

3 fresh bay leaves

1 cup red wine

2 cups cannellini beans, soaked in cold water overnight (or 2 x 400 g cans)

1 tablespoon finely chopped rosemary leaves

2 x 400 g cans chopped tomatoes in juice

3 tablespoons tomato paste

1½ cups water

salt and freshly ground black pepper

Preheat the oven to 180°C.

Heat the olive oil in a large casserole dish and cook the onion and garlic for about 5 minutes. Add the sausages whole, or you can squeeze out the sausage meat from the skins. Cook until browned — about 8–10 minutes more. Stir often.

Add the bay leaves, wine, drained beans, rosemary, tomatoes and tomato paste. Pour in the water and season with salt and lots of pepper.

Bring the casserole to the boil, then cover with a lid and transfer to the oven. Bake for 2 hours, stirring often, until the beans are cooked. If using canned beans, these are already cooked so you need only bake for 1 hour. Serve in bowls with crusty bread.

It's such a pleasure spending time in the kitchen with Mamma. We share the same philosophy — making wonderful dishes out of seasonal produce — using up all the leftovers with a no-waste policy.

Desserts

Tiramisu is one of the best-known Italian desserts, and the flavour variations are numerous. Mamma sometimes uses Frangelico hazelnut liqueur instead of Tia Maria. I usually put a layer of whipped cream on the top of my dish and grate chocolate over that.

Mamma used Vincenzo sponge finger biscuits, which are available in New Zealand at delis and specialty food stores, although other brands work just as well.

Tiramisu

Serves 10–12

7 large, very fresh eggs — still warm
  from the hen if possible!

¾ cup caster sugar

1 cup coffee liqueur, such as
  Tia Maria or Kahlúa

400 g mascarpone

1½ cups strong espresso

60 sponge fingers (Savoiardi biscuits)

whipped cream to serve, if desired

dark chocolate to grate

Separate the eggs. Beat the egg yolks, sugar and 1 tablespoon of the coffee liqueur until thick, pale and creamy. All the sugar should be dissolved. Add the mascarpone and beat until thick and smooth.

Separately, beat the egg whites until frothy. Fold the beaten egg whites into the mascarpone mixture.

Mix the espresso and remaining liqueur together in a small bowl. Quickly dunk each sponge finger biscuit into the coffee mixture and arrange them in a layer on the base of a 20 x 30 cm lasagne-style dish. Top with a layer of mascarpone cream. Alternate sponge fingers and mascarpone, finishing with a mascarpone layer followed by a layer of whipped cream (if desired). Sprinkle with finely grated dark chocolate, or Mamma sometimes uses a sprinkling of drinking chocolate powder. Leave in the fridge for at least 3 hours before serving.

Minted & Sugared Fresh Pineapple

Serves 6

1 fresh pineapple
½ cup caster sugar
large handful mint leaves, washed
  and finely sliced

Peel and chop the pineapple into small pieces, or dice until it almost looks like crushed pineapple. Remove any of the coarse core pieces. Sprinkle with the caster sugar and mint. Toss to coat well then leave, covered, in the refrigerator for at least an hour for the flavours to diffuse and the sugar to dissolve.

Serve in small glass dishes or wine glasses.

Rosewater Panna Cotta

Makes 6

3 sheets titanium-strength gelatine
1½ cups (375 ml) milk
1½ cups (375 ml) cream
¾ cup caster sugar
2 tablespoons rosewater
fresh fruit to serve
rose petals to garnish

Soak the gelatine sheets in cold water.

Bring the milk, cream and caster sugar to the boil, then remove from heat. Lift the gelatine sheets out of the water, removing any excess liquid. Add to the cream mixture, stirring until the gelatine has dissolved. Stir in the rosewater and pour the mixture through a fine sieve into a jug.

Pour into 6 half-cup (approximately 125 ml) dariole moulds or ramekins. Refrigerate for at least 6 hours. (These can be made the day before serving.)

To serve, run a small knife around the edge of the mould, then stand it in boiling water for 4–5 seconds. Place a plate over the mould, then flip both over so the plate is underneath. Carefully lift off the mould.

Serve with fresh fruit and garnish with rose petals.

Strawberries with Balsamic

Drizzle a splash of balsamic vinegar over hulled fresh strawberries. Add a dusting of caster sugar if they are not a really sweet variety.

Serve with a dollop of mascarpone.

Chianti Granita

Serves 4

2 cups Chianti
grated rind and juice of 2 oranges
¾ cup sugar
2½ cups water

Place all the ingredients in a medium saucepan and bring to a simmer for 10 minutes. Cool to room temperature, then chill the mixture. Freeze in a metal dish such as a cake tin, so that the mixture is no more than 5–6 cm deep.

When frozen, scrape with a metal spoon into icy shards and serve in glasses with a parfait spoon.

Fichi al Forno (Baked Figs)

Serves 6

24 firm but ripe figs
¾ cup caster sugar
¼ cup brandy or rum
grated rind of 1 orange
mascarpone to serve

Preheat oven to 180°C. Spray a large ovenproof dish or roasting tray with non-stick baking spray.

Wash the figs, then cut from the top as if into quarters, but stop halfway down the figs. Place in the prepared dish then sprinkle with the sugar, brandy and orange rind. Bake for 15 minutes. Serve hot with mascarpone.

Blueberry Custard Crema

Serves 4

For the crema
500 ml full-cream milk
1 teaspoon vanilla
4 egg yolks
½ cup caster sugar

For the blueberries
2 cups blueberries
1 tablespoon caster sugar
2 tablespoons water

crème fraîche to serve

Heat the milk and vanilla until boiling.

Beat the egg yolks and caster sugar together until pale and creamy. Continue beating while you add the hot milk and vanilla to the egg mixture. Beat until smoothly combined. Return to the saucepan and gently heat until thickened, stirring constantly. Do not boil. Remove from heat and cool.

In a saucepan, heat the blueberries with the sugar and water until boiling. Simmer, stirring often, for about 10 minutes until they are a jammy, syrupy consistency.

Pour the cooled custard into glasses. Serve well chilled, topped with blueberries and a dollop of crème fraîche on the top.

Mandarin & Prosecco Jellies

Serves 6

700 ml mandarin juice
2 teaspoons grated mandarin rind
300 ml Prosecco
4 sheets titanium-strength gelatine
extra mandarin to garnish
Prosecco to serve

Place the mandarin juice and rind in a small saucepan. Add the Prosecco and gently heat until almost boiling. Remove from heat.

Soak the leaves of gelatine in cold water until soft and rubbery. Lift the gelatine sheets out of the water, dripping off any excess. Stir the gelatine into the hot mandarin juice until the sheets have dissolved.

Cool the liquid for 15 minutes then pour into wine glasses or small dishes. Set in the fridge.

Serve chilled with a few slices of mandarin to garnish and glasses of Prosecco.

Spiced Amaretto Oranges & Orange & Cinnamon Gelato

Serves 4–6

For the Spiced Amaretto Oranges
100 ml Amaretto liqueur
¼ cup caster sugar
10 black peppercorns
4 cloves
4 cardamom pods
grated rind of 4 oranges
6 whole oranges, carefully peeled to
   remove all the white pith, then sliced

For the Orange & Cinnamon Gelato
1 litre full-cream milk
grated rind of 2 oranges
1½ teaspoons cinnamon
6 egg yolks
1¼ cups caster sugar

To make the Spiced Amaretto Oranges

Combine the Amaretto, sugar, spices and orange rind in a small saucepan. Stir over a low heat until the sugar has dissolved, then bring to the boil. Simmer until the mixture thickens and is quite syrupy — about 5 minutes.

Strain cooled mixture over the sliced oranges and chill.

To make the Gelato

Place the milk, orange rind and cinnamon in a medium saucepan and bring to the boil. Turn the heat down and simmer for 5 minutes, then remove from the heat.

Whisk the egg yolks and caster sugar together until pale and creamy. Add the milk mixture to the eggs and mix until well combined. Return the mixture to the saucepan and stir over a gentle heat until it thickens and coats the back of a spoon. Do not boil.

Cool to room temperature, then pour into an ice-cream churn. Follow the manufacturer's instructions and freeze.

This sounds like a crazy combination but it's actually a fantastic explosion of flavour — a real 'fire and ice' experience.

Lime & Black Pepper Ice

Serves 6

grated rind and juice of 6 limes
2 cups sugar
1 litre buttermilk
1 tablespoon freshly ground black
  pepper
lime slices to garnish

Stir all the ingredients over medium heat in a large saucepan. Stir to dissolve the sugar, then cool to room temperature and pour into an ice-cream churn. Follow the manufacturer's instructions and freeze.

Serve in small martini or wine glasses, garnish with lime slices and eat using long parfait spoons.

If you don't have a chef's blowtorch, make this in ovenproof bowls and place them under a preheated hot grill to achieve the caramelised effect.

Summer Berry Gratin

Serves 6

2 cups fresh raspberries
2 cups sliced fresh strawberries
2 cups blueberries or blackberries
¾ cup caster sugar
500 g mascarpone

Place the berries in 6 small dishes or bowls. Sprinkle a teaspoon or 2 of caster sugar over the berries and mix through.

Divide the mascarpone into 6 portions and dollop over the berries, smoothing it down with the back of a spoon to cover as much of the surface as possible. Sprinkle the remaining caster sugar over the top of the mascarpone.

Using a chef's blowtorch, caramelise the sugar until it is melted and bubbling and golden brown. Serve immediately.

Mamma uses a sour morello or sharp cherry jam, but you could substitute other flavours.

Crostata di Visciole (Cherry Tart)

Serves 8–12

3¼ cups flour
1 cup caster sugar
pinch salt
75 g cold butter, cubed
75 g lard, cubed
3 eggs
grated rind of 1 orange
1½ cups cherry jam
1 egg yolk, mixed with 1 teaspoon cold water
icing sugar to dust
whipped cream to serve

Preheat the oven to 175°C. Spray a 28–30 cm shallow, loose-bottomed flan tin with non-stick baking spray.

Mix the flour, sugar and salt together in a bowl. Rub in the butter and lard cubes until the mixture resembles breadcrumbs, then mix in the eggs and orange rind, kneading to combine into a soft dough.

Roll out the pastry on a well-floured surface and line the base of the tin with two-thirds of the pastry. Place in the fridge. Roll out the remaining dough and use a pastry or ravioli wheel to cut into 2 cm strips.

Spread the jam over the cooled pastry base. Make a lattice top over the jam layer with the strips. Brush these with the egg wash and bake for 45–50 minutes until the pastry is cooked and golden.

Leave to cool in the tin, then carefully remove to a serving platter.

Dust with icing sugar and serve with whipped cream.

Grilled Nectarines with Amaretto

Serves 8

8 large nectarines
3 tablespoons caster sugar
1 teaspoon ground cinnamon
1 teaspoon vanilla bean paste
150 ml Amaretto
mascarpone to serve

Preheat the grill.

Slice the nectarines in half and remove the stones. Place in a roasting dish.

Mix together the sugar, cinnamon, vanilla bean paste and Amaretto. Drizzle over the nectarine halves. Grill for 15 minutes. Serve with the mascarpone.

Italian food is about time-honoured traditions: feet firmly in family, love of the land and God's seasons, and pride in making by hand.

Baking

Amaretti Biscuits

Makes 35

4 egg whites
1 cup caster sugar
2¾ cups ground almonds
½ teaspoon almond essence
½ cup icing sugar, plus extra to dust

Preheat the oven to 110°C. Line 2 oven trays with non-stick baking paper.

Using an electric mixer, beat the egg whites until soft peaks form. Very slowly, a teaspoon at a time, add the sugar while running the machine on full speed. Beat until the meringue is thick and glossy, with no trace of grittiness. Slow the mixer to its lowest speed and add the ground almonds, almond essence and icing sugar.

Spoon into a piping bag fitted with a plain nozzle about 1.5 cm wide. Pipe out 4–5 cm lengths of mixture onto the prepared trays. Dust with extra icing sugar and bake for 35–40 minutes until very light golden brown, crisp and dry. Cool on the tray. Serve with espresso.

Store in an airtight container.

Fiorentini (Florentines)

Makes 20

125 g butter

¾ cup caster sugar

2 tablespoons milk

4 tablespoons flour

½ cup flaked almonds, chopped

½ cup crystallised mixed peel, finely chopped

¼ cup currants

¼ cup sultanas

10 glacé cherries, chopped

200 g dark chocolate

Preheat the oven to 180°C. Line 2 oven trays with non-stick baking paper. Spray the paper with non-stick baking spray.

Place the butter in a small saucepan and melt. Add the sugar and milk. Bring to the boil, stirring to dissolve the sugar. Boil for 1 minute then remove from heat. Add the flour, almonds and fruit. Mix well.

Place teaspoons of mixture onto the prepared trays, leaving room around each pile to allow them to spread. Flatten the piles and bake for 10–12 minutes until golden. Cool for a few minutes on the tray then transfer to a wire rack and cool completely.

Trim to a nice round shape — I use kitchen scissors for this. Melt the chocolate and spread over the flat side of the Florentines. Using a fork, make wavy stripes in the chocolate and allow to set.

Store in an airtight container.

This is a delicious, moist dessert-type cake. It is fabulous if you have fresh apricots, but I've successfully made it with canned apricots too.

Torta di Albicocche (Pistachio & Apricot Cake)

Serves 6–8

800 g apricots (approximately 10),
  or 2 x 400 g cans apricots, drained
200 g butter
1¼ cups caster sugar
1 teaspoon vanilla
5 eggs
2 cups self-raising flour
½ cup shelled pistachio nuts
softly whipped cream, apricot yoghurt
  or mascarpone to serve

Preheat the oven to 190°C. Spray a 23 cm springform tin with non-stick baking spray and line the base with non-stick baking paper.

Place the apricots in a large bowl and cover with boiling water. Wait for 2 minutes, then drain and peel off the skins. Halve the apricots, discard the stones, then cut again into quarters.

Beat the butter and caster sugar together until pale and creamy. Add the vanilla, then mix in the eggs, 1 at a time. Add the flour and stir through the apricot pieces. Pour the mixture into the prepared tin and sprinkle the surface with pistachio nuts. Bake for 55–60 minutes until firm in the centre.

Cool in the tin for 10 minutes, then carefully remove and cool on a wire rack. Serve with softly whipped cream, apricot yoghurt or mascarpone.

Panforte di Siena (Siena Cake)

Makes 15–18 slices

1 cup blanched almonds
1 cup hazelnuts
150 g mixed peel
100 g dark chocolate
¾ cup flour
3 tablespoons baking cocoa — the best
 quality you can get
2 teaspoons ground cinnamon
¼ cup sugar
½ cup honey
¼ cup water
icing sugar to dust

Preheat the oven to 160°C. Line a 20 cm round tin with non-stick baking paper.

Roughly chop the almonds and place in a shallow baking tray. Place in the oven and roast for about 10 minutes. Roast the hazelnuts in a separate tray for slightly longer — around 15 minutes — then rub off their skins with a clean tea towel. Discard the skins and chop roughly.

Chop up the mixed peel and chocolate. Sift the flour, cocoa and cinnamon into a medium-sized bowl. Mix in the nuts, peel and chocolate.

Place the sugar, honey and water in a small saucepan and stir over a low heat until the sugar is dissolved. Just swirling the pan rather than stirring it, boil until it reaches 116°C on a sugar thermometer.

Pour the boiling liquid into the other ingredients and mix thoroughly. Transfer to the prepared tin, pressing down firmly and smoothing the surface with a wet spoon.

Bake for 35–40 minutes. It may still look a little underdone but don't be tempted to overcook it. Cool completely in the tin before attempting to remove.

Dust with icing sugar and cut with a sharp knife into very thin wedges.

This is a delightfully moist apple cake, perfect for dessert and made extra tasty by golden delicious apples and a sharp little zing of lemon. It also reheats beautifully.

Apple & Lemon Torta

Serves 8

5–6 golden delicious apples
 (approximately 700 g)
grated rind and juice of 1 lemon
4 eggs
¾ cup caster sugar
1¼ cups flour
1 teaspoon baking powder
¼ teaspoon salt
125 g butter, melted and cooled
softly whipped cream, lemon yoghurt
 or mascarpone to serve

Preheat the oven to 180°C. Spray a 23 cm springform tin with non-stick baking spray and line the base with non-stick baking paper.

Peel, core and quarter the apples and slice thinly — a mandolin is very useful to get lovely even slices. Place the apple slices in a bowl with the lemon rind and juice. Stir to coat each apple slice with the lemon.

Using a hand-held electric beater, whisk the eggs and sugar together until really pale, creamy and thick. Sift the flour, baking powder and salt into the egg mixture. Add the melted butter and lightly fold together. Fold in the apple and lemon and spoon into the prepared tin.

Bake for 45–50 minutes until a skewer inserted in the centre of the cake comes out clean. Cool for 15 minutes in the tin, then carefully remove the sides of the tin and turn out, right side up, onto a wire rack to cool completely.

Serve with softly whipped cream, lemon yoghurt or mascarpone.

Mamma serves these with dessert wine — you actually dunk them into the wine like gingernut biscuits into your tea. Cranberries, dried cherries, other nuts and chocolate can be substituted for the raisins and pinenuts.

Raisin & Pinenut Biscotti

Makes about 20

¾ cup brown sugar
1 egg, plus 1 egg yolk
1¼ cups flour
½ teaspoon salt
1 teaspoon allspice
½ cup raisins
½ cup pinenuts

Preheat the oven to 180°C. Line an oven tray with non-stick baking paper.

Beat the sugar, egg and egg yolk together until pale and thick. Add the flour, salt and allspice and mix well. Add the raisins and pinenuts.

Shape the mixture into a roll about 28 cm long. Press to flatten slightly.

Place the log on the prepared tray and bake for 20–25 minutes until golden. Cool for 5 minutes, then cut into slices about 1 cm thick with a bread knife. Lay the slices flat on the oven tray and bake for a further 10 minutes. Cool on a wire rack.

Store in an airtight container when cold.

These are delicious deep-fried crispy pastries to eat with coffee.

Crostoli

Makes 20

1 egg
1 tablespoon caster sugar
1 tablespoon Marsala wine, or sherry
2 tablespoons milk
1 tablespoon butter, softened
grated rind of 1 lemon
1½ cups flour
vegetable oil for frying
icing sugar to dust

Whisk the egg and caster sugar together in a small bowl until pale and frothy. Add the Marsala, milk, butter and lemon rind. Add 1 cup of flour and mix well, then slowly add the remaining flour until the dough is coming away from the sides of the bowl. Depending on the size of the egg, you may not need all of the flour — just proceed slowly until the dough has reached the desired consistency.

Turn out the dough onto a floured surface and roll out to 2 mm thick. (Dust the dough and rolling pin with lots of flour to prevent sticking.) Using a pastry wheel, cut into 3 x 8 cm long strips — about the size of a Weetbix.

Heat the oil to 180°C.

Deep fry the pastry for 2–3 minutes in batches, turning to cook evenly. Cook until they are a lovely golden brown colour and very crispy. Drain on paper towels and sprinkle generously with icing sugar. Serve warm.

Torrone is an Italian nougat treat, usually more brittle and a little harder than French nougat. It seems complicated to make but as long as you have an accurate sugar thermometer it is great — both delicious and impressive. Liquid glucose is available in the sugar section of good supermarkets, and confectionery rice paper to line the tin is available at good chef and kitchen supply stores or delis.

Pistachio Torrone

Makes 36 pieces

2 cups sugar
1 cup liquid glucose
½ cup honey
2 egg whites
1 teaspoon vanilla
1 cup pistachio nuts, peeled and chopped

Line the bottom of an 18 cm square tin with confectionery rice paper and spray the sides with non-stick baking spray.

Mix together the sugar, liquid glucose and honey in a medium-large saucepan and stir over low heat until the sugar crystals have dissolved. Increase the heat and, while stirring, gently boil until the mixture reaches 130°C on a sugar thermometer.

Using an electric mixer, beat the egg whites to firm peaks and slowly and carefully, with the mixer running, add half the syrup. Add the vanilla and keep the mixer running on low speed. Return the remainder of the syrup to the heat and boil until it reaches 154°C on a sugar thermometer. This should take a further 7–8 minutes of boiling.

Very carefully add this hot syrup to the mixer and beat until glossy and thick. Stir through the pistachios, then scrape into the prepared tin. Smooth the surface and press a sheet of rice paper onto the surface.

Cool completely before cutting with a sharp knife into bite-sized pieces. Wrap in plastic wrap or cellophane. It will store in an airtight container for up to three weeks.

Drinks

Prosecco with Fresh Figs

Place gorgeous, small, ripe fresh figs or halved larger figs into chilled flutes or wine glasses. Pour over icy cold Prosecco (or other sparkling wine) and enjoy. Drink the Prosecco, then eat the deliciously sozzled fig.

Peach Bellinis

Peel and slice ripe peaches — preferably the white-fleshed variety — and place in the bottom of champagne flutes or wine glasses. Squish with a fork to release a bit of juice and fill with chilled Prosecco or sparkling white wine.

A spoon or 2 of bottled peach juice or purée can be used instead of fresh peaches and, at a push, canned peaches will work out just fine as well.

This is Papà's special recipe and the best limoncello I've ever tried. It is quite easy to make but you have to produce it over a couple of days, then wait at least a few days until you can drink it. It is worth the wait!

To get the correct sharp lemon flavour, you need to use true Italian lemons such as Villa Franca, Lisbon or Yen Ben. Don't use Meyer lemons, which are a hybrid of a mandarin. Only the peel of the lemons is used for this recipe, not the juice, which can be squeezed and frozen. Papà uses pure alcohol available from the chemist in Italy, but I've successfully made it with vodka.

Papà's Limoncello

10 lemons
1 litre alcohol
800 g sugar
1 litre water

Day one

Carefully peel the lemons. Papà used a little knife but a microplane works a treat, or you can use a potato peeler. It is important not to get any pith — the white bit — in the mix.

Add the alcohol. Cover the bowl with a cloth and allow to infuse for 24 hours.

Day two

Add the sugar to 1 litre of water and bring to the boil, stirring until the sugar has dissolved. Cool.

Strain the alcohol to remove the lemon rind, which can be discarded. Mix the cooled sugar syrup and lemon alcohol together.

Limoncello is best 2–3 days after making, and can be stored for much longer — up to a month. Keep it in the freezer and serve very cold over ice with soda. It won't freeze solid because of the alcohol content.

Affogato

Serve each guest a small bowl of vanilla ice cream with a shot glass of espresso and a shot glass of Frangelico or other liqueur.

Pour the shots over the ice cream.

Acknowledgements

Special thanks to the wonderful Jae Frew — fabulous and favourite photographer and book designer (and friend).

To Simona, Said, Cameron, Beverley and Marina, who make our Italian stay at Villa Campo Verde so special and unique.

To Pam and Bruce Young of House of Travel. Not only wonderful travel agents but such great supporters of Hospice New Zealand.

Thanks to Thomas at Emirates, who looks after us so well. Susan (Angel), our fabulous stylist. Patrina (Patch) for help with the design and layout of the book. Emily, my right hand in the cook-school kitchen. The staff at Seagars at Oxford.

To Jenny Hellen and her team at Random House.

Thank you to Dawn and Richard Sparks of the Northbrook Colonial Museum in Rangiora.

And, as always, to my Darling Rosso — couldn't do this without you.

Essential Weights & Measures

Working out the different wordings and quantities in recipes can become a bit of a minefield. Here is a useful list of conversions.

Temperature Conversions

Description	Celsius	Fahrenheit
Cool oven	110°C	225°F
Very low oven	150°C	300°F
Moderate oven	180°C	350°F
Hot oven	220°C	425°F
Very hot oven	230°C	450°F

Liquid Conversions

5 ml	1 teaspoon
15 ml	1 tablespoon
250 ml	1 cup
600 ml	1 pint
1000 ml / 1 litre	1⅔ pints

NB: The Australian metric tablespoon measures 20 ml.

Length Conversions

2.5 cm	1 inch
12 cm	4½ inches
20 cm	8 inches
24 cm	9½ inches
30 cm	12 inches

Ingredients

butter	100 g	1 American stick
	225 g	1 cup
	30 g	2 tablespoons
cheese	115 g	1 cup grated tasty
	150 g	1 cup grated parmesan
egg whites	1 large (size 8) egg white 55 ml or 30 g	
flour	150 g	1 cup
golden syrup or honey	350 g	1 cup
onions	115 g	1 cup, chopped
rice	200 g	1 cup uncooked rice
	165 g	1 cup cooked rice
sugar	225 g	1 cup caster or granulated sugar
	200 g	1 cup brown sugar
	125 g	1 cup icing sugar

Ingredients' Common Names

aubergine	eggplant
baking paper	parchment paper, silicone paper
cannellini beans	white kidney beans
peppers	capsicums, bell peppers
coriander	cilantro
spring onions	green onions, scallions
fillet (of meat)	tenderloin
icing sugar	confectioners' sugar
rocket	arugula, roquette
courgette	zucchini

Special equipment used in this book such as pasta machines, sugar thermometers, Magimixes, measuring cups etc are available to buy online at www.joseagar.com

Umbrian Cook School

At the very heart of my Italian Cooking School experience are some truly amazing people who, over the years, have become a part of our beautiful Italian 'family' including Mamma and Papà, Simona, Said and Marina.

Only in Italy will you find such a passion for food: truffles that will be carefully prepared and served, tomatoes that are without a doubt the tastiest on the planet and huge tins of olive oil that will make their contribution in the creation of an exquisite meal — made all the more enjoyable because we helped to create it.

No modern appliances or pre-packaged foods are found here and, in their place, natural foods are prepared in a daily ritual that has existed for centuries.

Meanwhile we can enjoy some Italian lessons with Mamma's lovely daughter Simona and at siesta time we all meet around the pool of our amazing villa to share our experiences of the day — bliss.

There's always something to do: maybe an evening at the local opera or a visit to one of our favourite nearby towns — Montefalco with lunch at Antonelli Winery, or the town of Spoleto — a market town and a great place to sample the local coffee and chocolates. Then there's Castelluccio, famous for its lentils and a great place for a picnic in the hills.

This opportunity to experience a culture dominated by fine food and wine in the heartland of Italian cooking is only available at House of Travel. The tour coordinator is Pamela Young. If you would love to join us please contact Pam at pammy@hot.co.nz

HOUSE OF TRAVEL

Simona & Said —
A Love Story

Simona is Mamma's daughter and our Italian teacher/translator.
Said is her Moroccan husband. Simona tells the story of meeting
Said for the first time.

As soon as I stepped inside the hotel, a traditional casbah right in front of the wonderful
dunes, I saw Said and felt there was something special about him. It was the way he
moved, his grace in doing everything, his calm, gentle, reserved manners: he seemed
someone deeply at peace with himself, someone pure in a way we have forgotten. To me
he looked so noble that I secretly nicknamed him 'The Prince of the Desert'. Yes, I had
fallen in love. And not only with him; I had fallen in love with the desert and the Berbers,
with their sweet little village in front of the dunes, their simple but dignified way of
life, with their open minds and pure hearts, the calm rhythms of their daily life, the vast
spaces, the amazing colours, the silences of the desert, the incredibly brilliant stars at
night. I loved them immediately, their nobility, their dignity, their honesty conquered my
heart, and Said is the person who most embodies this.

Now that we live together in Umbria he has not changed at all. It was very difficult for
me to bring him to Italy as Moroccans who haven't got a regular job cannot leave their
country to come to Europe. So we went through two years of hope and disappointment
but in the end he's now here with me! Everyone has come to recognise his wonderful
qualities. After all, he's The Prince of the Desert!

Index